THE STOOGES' LOST EPISODES

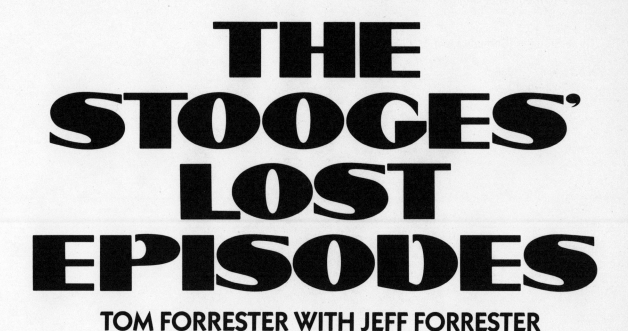

THE STOOGES' LOST EPISODES

TOM FORRESTER WITH JEFF FORRESTER

CONTEMPORARY
BOOKS

CHICAGO · NEW YORK

Library of Congress Cataloging-in-Publication Data

Forrester, Tom.
    The Stooges' lost episodes : the 50 never-before-released Stooge adventures / Tom Forrester with Jeff Forrester.
       p.   cm.
    ISBN 0-8092-4655-4
    1. Three Stooges (Comedy team)   I. Forrester, Jeffrey.
II. Title.
PN1995.9.T5F69   1988
791.43'028'0922—dc19   87-35225
                                      CIP

Published by Contemporary Books, Inc.
180 North Michigan Avenue, Chicago, Illinois 60601
Manufactured in the United States of America
Library of Congress Catalog Card Number: 87-35225
International Standard Book Number: 0-8092-4655-4

Published simultaneously in Canada by Beaverbooks, Ltd.
195 Allstate Parkway, Valleywood Business Park
Markham, Ontario L3R 4T8 Canada

To Don and Ruth

Contents

Preface:
A Few Words About the Stooges

The unearthing of these previously thought-to-be "lost" Three Stooges films has resulted in a worldwide upheaval in Stooge thinking. Here, then, are the comments, criticisms, and opinions of some of the entertainment industry's leading performers on the subject of Stooges. . . .

"Yes, I had the Stooges on my show several times. I was too busy doing other things to stop and talk with them."　　—Steve Allen

"The only thing I ever learned from them was how to duck."　　—Lucille Ball

"Sure, I used to know the Three Stooges. . . . But that was a hundred years ago."　　　　　—George Burns

"Just once I'd have liked to turn, look at the Stooges, and say, are you men *sure* you know what you're doing?"　—John Candy

"I played golf with them once . . . what a mistake."　　　　　　—Tim Conway

"It's nice that the Stooges got paid to do the same kind of stuff in the movies that they did around the house."　—Bill Cosby

"When we were kids, my father used to change the channel from Three Stooges to Laurel and Hardy. I'll always be indebted to him for that."　　　—Billy Crystal

"Call me up some time and I'll tell you a hundred stories about Ted Healy and the Three Stooges."　　　　—Bob Hope

"Men only like the Three Stooges. Women, for some reason, can't stand them. But if you ask any guy who the three most important people in American history are, they'll tell you (1) George Washington, (2) Abraham Lincoln, and (3) Moe."　—Jay Leno

"The Three Stooges were very awkward, completely graceless comedians. It was the sound effects and the schtick that sold them."　　　　　—Jerry Lewis

"We don't really emulate the Stooges. I don't think we could bring ourselves up to that level of sophistication." —Steve Martin

"Oh, the Three Stooges. God, yes. They were marvelous."　—Larry "Bud" Melman

"When I was a kid, I thought the Three Stooges were the funniest thing in the world . . . then I grew up."　—Bill Murray

11

Acknowledgments

The authors wish to thank the following individuals without whose help this book would not have been possible:

Edward Bernds
Joe Besser
Steve Cox
Jean (Mrs. Joe) DeRita
Joe DeRita
Eddie Deezen
Moe Feinberg
Joe Franklin
Bob Frischmann
Henry Freulich
Mousie Garner
Mark Gilman, Jr.
Abby (Mrs. Dick) Hakins
Dick Hakins
Betty (Mrs. Ted) Healy
Babe (Mrs. Shemp) Howard

Jeff Lenburg
David Maska
Sidney Miller
Benny Rubin
James Shemansky
Samuel Sherman
Emil Sitka
Dave Stuckey
Elwood Ullman
Jack White
Jules White
Paul Winchell
Sammy Wolf

All photographs courtesy of the Steve Cox Collection. Illustrations by Gordon Parker. Interviews and research for the chapter on "The Three Stooges Scrapbook" conducted by Steve Cox.

Introduction:
A Guide to the Stooges' Lost Episodes

The genesis of *The Stooges' Lost Episodes* was a conversation over dinner exactly ten years ago. When the authors were in Hollywood conducting an interview with the Stooges' longtime pal Emil Sitka in 1978 for another book project, they were startled to learn of a Three Stooges "pilot" film that had been produced in the late 1940s. They were further surprised to discover that the Stooges had made many television appearances throughout their lengthy career, most of which had never resurfaced in reruns.

Subsequent digging and research indicated that there were also Stooges *movies* that had never aired on TV. And then there were rumors that actual footage from episodes already in release had disappeared, scissored out of the 16-millimeter TV prints of the Stooges' old two-reelers originally released in syndication in the late 1950s.

The subject of "lost" Stooges footage was an intriguing one, but hardly intriguing enough to warrant writing an uncontracted-for book. After all, even if such footage was eventually "found," what would be the point of discussing it or describing it if no one would ever get the opportunity to *see* it?

This, of course, was ten long years ago. At least a few years before VCRs had become as widespread amongst consumers as television itself had become by the mid-1950s. And a good many years before these previously "lost" episodes actually began resurfacing through release by video distributors as mighty as Columbia Pictures and as minuscule as Madhouse Video.

Today, virtually every Stoogemaniac owns a home video recorder. And a surprising number of formerly "lost" Stooges films, originally made for theatrical or television release, have been re-released (or released for the first time ever) in videocassette form. At last, demand met supply. The Stooges' lost episodes, no longer the exclusive booty of moneyed film collectors, had finally become available to the average Joe. And thus, *The Stooges' Lost Episodes* was born.

Now Stooge fanatics can enjoy the antics of their favorite threesome in dozens of appearances that, for the most part, have not been in general release of any kind for a long, long time.

Much of this material is quite surprising—appearances from the beginning of the trio's film career all the way to the very end have turned up, with representative stuff in between.

But, like the Stooges' long-running series of Columbia two-reel comedies, their batting average in the "lost" episodes remains about the same. Some are good, some are bad, and most of them are mediocre. Since the Stooges never held a grip on the creative rein of their films, what resulted was hit-and-miss product that depended more on the particular director or writer involved than on the efforts of the Stooges themselves.

For example, the Stooges absolutely hated working with a director named Harry Edwards. A former associate of both Frank Capra's and Harry Langdon's, Edwards was a brilliant comedy writer-director who also drank too much, and, as a result, his work was often slipshod. However, of the two films he directed with the Stooges, his first effort, *Matri-Phony* (1942), is perhaps one of the trio's all-time funniest entries, and his second, *Three Little Twirps* (1943) isn't bad, either. On the other hand, the Stooges enjoyed working with a director named Preston Black (also known as Jack White), who helmed what was one of the team's personal favorites, *A Pain in the Pullman* (1936), amongst several others. However, the majority of Black/White's films with the Stooges are probably the least inspired in the series, with *Pullman* standing out as a particularly tedious endeavor.

The Stooges' all-time favorite writer-director, though, was Edward Bernds, who started out as a sound man on their films in the 1930s and began working with them creatively in 1944. The team loved working with Bernds, whose affable personality and vast experience lent itself to the Stooges' workmanlike approach. In addition, Bernds also happened to be an excellent comedy director, and, consequently, the films he turned out with the Stooges represent their very best work.

It's pretty clear that the boys were completely at the mercy of their producers, directors, and writers, and, since the majority of the "lost episodes" aren't directed by sympathetic craftsmen like Bernds, the quality level is wildly erratic. However, there are "lost" films like *Meet the Baron* (1933) and *Time Out for Rhythm* (1941) that showcase the Stooges in a framework that is near-perfect for their improvisational clowning. In addition, the curiosity value of seeing the Stooges in early TV pilots, as guest stars on live TV programs, and cutting up in home-movie footage from the 1940s is enough to warrant the interest of even the moderately manic Stoogephile.

So the Stooges' lost episodes represent not so much a treasure trove of classic comedy as a few more pieces to the jigsaw puzzle that was the team's multi-media career.

In that respect, *The Stooges' Lost Episodes* is not meant to be the last word on newly found Stooges footage. It couldn't possibly attempt to be, if only because there is new footage turning up every day, and more and more material is being released on home video and through television airings with each passing month. Instead, *Lost Episodes* is intended as a guidebook to assist Stoogemaniacs in getting their hands on that "lost" stuff that *is* now available. In addition, the authors have included a filmography that lists the lost episodes of the Three Stooges—both collectively and individually—to serve as a checklist of sorts. The majority of the films are not yet available, but that doesn't mean they won't be in the very near future.

In fact, future editions of this book might even require a chapter on "made-for-TV" Three Stooges movies—"Entertainment Tonight" recently reported that plans are underway to produce a two-hour television feature chronicling the lives of Moe, Larry, and Curly, complete with three actors essaying the roles of the high priests of low comedy.

It's revelations like these that indicate the public's obsession with the Three Stooges is going to be around for a long, long time. It also makes all the more real the possibility that more and more "lost" episodes might be coming out of the woodwork.

So—without further ado—it is our sincere wish that you enjoy reading *The Stooges' Lost Episodes* as much as we enjoyed collecting the advance money for it.

THE STOOGES' LOST EPISODES

Lost Anecdote #1
"If a Body Meets a Buddy"

Believe it or not, comedian Buddy Hackett was once asked to audition for the Three Stooges—he was actually one of Moe Howard's personal favorites.

"I dropped by where they were rehearsing, and they were banging each other around and hitting each other over the head with great big pipes and everything. I took one look at that and said, 'Nope!'"

As a guest on "The Tonight Show" in 1986, Hackett said, "The reason I couldn't join them was I couldn't do *this*," at which point he proceeded to imitate Curly, screaming and throwing himself about in his chair.

Chapter One: "Why Not Four Stooges? I Know a Guy Who Plays a Mean Xylophone!"

The first Stooges "lost episode" is also their first movie, period. And, unless you're a diehard Stooges fan with an extensive knowledge of trivia, you might be surprised to learn that it featured four—not three—Stooges. Here's the story:

In 1930, the Stooges were actually part of a vaudeville comedy team called Ted Healy and His Racketeers. Healy was a standup comedian who employed his boyhood pal Moe Howard, his brother Shemp, and their acquaintance Larry Fine as "stooges," or "second bananas." By the early 1930s, Healy was calling them his Racketeers, and the foursome was headlining the bill at the old Palace Theatre in New York. For a comedian in those days, starring at the Palace was as prestigious as appearing on "The Tonight Show" would be fifty years later. It was the top of the line, *the* place to be seen. Also sharing the bill with Healy and the Racketeers was Freddie "Pansy" Sanborn, a goofball comedian who played xylophone. "Pansy" occasionally participated in sketches with Healy, thus providing the legendary Ted with four Stooges instead of just three.

Healy was brilliantly entertaining, an inventive performer who could "wow 'em" with a Jolsonesque song-and-dance number one minute and "slay 'em" with a wildly improvised routine the next. His Stooges were raucous, weird-looking, violent, and unsophisticated. Bizarre with a capital "B." Together, they were a smash, and they played to packed houses night after night.

Well, as the story goes, on one of these standing-room-only nights, a talent scout from Fox Studios in Hollywood dropped by the Palace to catch the show. He was taken with Healy and the Stooges. They were taken with the notion of moving to California and working in the movies. The next day, a deal was struck and Healy, the Stooges, and Freddie Sanborn—now a full-fledged Racketeer—were signed to star in their very first feature film, *Soup to Nuts*.

Soup to Nuts (1930) is a genuinely funny movie, and it's Healy's show all the way. The Stooges (or, in this case, Racketeers) have very, very little to do, but it is noteworthy if only because it was their first screen appearance together. In addition, the byplay between Healy and Shemp is wonderful, and is literally the only existing film of these two improvisational geniuses working together. Moe and Larry are amusing enough, while Freddie Sanborn, on the other hand, is painfully unfunny. It's pretty obvious they just brought him along from their Palace gig at Fox's insistence, because he never worked with the Stooges again.

"Pansy" is, however, an integral part of the group in *Soup to Nuts*—and what the Stooges do is mostly verbal, rather than physical, which is in itself somewhat surprising considering the plotline was concocted by Rube Goldberg, a cartoonist renowned for his love of visual humor. In addition, all four Stooges combed their hair straight back instead of relying on their traditional "wacky" haircuts. Was the comedy-haircut idea considered too "vaudeville" and not believable enough for the movies? Was this an attempt to "sophisticate" the

Stooges, to elevate their status from stage caricatures to full-fledged, flesh-and-blood human personalities? If so, the scheme obviously didn't take, for they reverted to their wild "do's" for their very next film appearance.

Even more peculiar than the idea of tampering with the Stooges' hairstyles is the fact that the boys don't even receive billing in the film's credits! This is disappoining, if for no other reason than that their scene with Healy is the highlight of the film.

20th Century–Fox, which owns the television rights to *Soup to Nuts*, says the film has been leased, along with a batch of other old movies, to WGN-TV in Chicago. Since WGN is now a cable superstation and is available in many parts of the country, you may want to check your TV listings for its television airing. At present, however, Fox has no plans for releasing the film on home video.

Ted Healy, relaxing among his fans in the early 1930s, shortly after the completion of *Soup to Nuts*.

Lost Anecdote #2
"So Long, Mr. Chaplin"

During the shooting of *Soup to Nuts*, Healy and the Stooges were visited on the set by a very special guest— the king of comedy himself, Charlie Chaplin. Ted and the Stooges were falling all over themselves trying to have their pictures taken with The Great Man. But according to Shemp's widow, Babe Howard, Healy managed to crowd the Stooges out of the limelight so only he wound up in any of the snapshots with Charlie! Shemp became terribly upset about the whole incident, because he idolized Chaplin and wanted to know what the master comedian-filmmaker thought about his brand of comedy.

After the photo session, Shemp struggled desperately to gain his attention, but the Little Tramp became distracted and left the set before Shemp even got a chance to tell Chaplin how much he thought of his work.

When it was all over, you can bet Shemp let Ted Healy know what he thought about *his* work.

Chapter Two:
"If You Think I'm Shaving My Head for a Movie, You're Nuts!"

After the release of *Soup to Nuts*, the Racketeers/Stooges found themselves a smash in the movies as well as on stage. According to Moe Howard, it was the Stooges—not Healy—who were offered a seven-year contract with Fox as a result. But Healy convinced Fox head Winnie Sheenan not to hire them, and the deal went down the drain. Moe, Larry, and Shemp were infuriated, and decided to go out on their own as Three Lost Souls—which was about what they were without Healy around to get them decent bookings.

Months pass. Healy threatens the Stooges with a lawsuit if they perform as a trio using "his" material. The Stooges tell him to get lost. Healy then threatens to leave a bomb in the Stooges' dressing room. The Stooges again tell him to get lost, but Shemp notices the reemergence of a childhood bed-wetting problem. Finally, Healy calms down. The boys decide to bury the hatchet—"forgive and forget." The act is now officially called, Ted Healy and His Stooges. Everything is exactly as it was before—with one major exception.

Shemp's wife refuses to let him rejoin. She can't stand Ted. He's obnoxious and manipulative, she says. "Ted would try to break them up all the time," says Babe Howard. "He'd try to get Shemp to sign without Moe and Larry, then Moe to sign without Shemp and Larry, then Larry to sign without Shemp and Moe . . . it was ridiculous. I told Shemp to forget about Ted, to go out on his own."

Which is exactly what Shemp did, quickly signing with Vitaphone Studios for his own series of "lost" episodes. Meanwhile, there's a vacancy amongst the Stooges. . . . Who's going to replace Shemp? Well, there's his fat kid brother, named Jerry, or something. Nice wavy hair. Moustache. Handsome kid. In fact, too normal-looking to be one of the Stooges.

"Sorry, pal," says Ted Healy, giving him the once-over, "you just don't cut the mustard."

Jerry Howard is heartbroken. This is his big chance to join the Stooges. To get into big-time vaudeville. And he's blown it because he's too damned handsome. He calls on Shemp, half in tears with frustration. Shemp will know what to do.

Boy, does Shemp know what to do! He drags

Jerry to the barbershop, sits him down in the chair, and instructs the barber to shave off all of Jerry's hair. "*You* heard me, shave it off!" says Shemp. A few minutes later, voila! Introducing Jerry "Curly" Howard, the newest would-be Stooge.

Jerry reauditions for Ted Healy. Healy loves him. He whispers to Moe, "Why didn't you show me this guy in the *first* place?"

Curly is in, and Ted and the Stooges are off to Hollywood for some personal appearances. And one brief appearance in a Paramount two-reeler called *Hollywood on Parade* (1933). No big deal, this film, except for one thing—it's Curly's first movie appearance. The first time Moe, Larry, and Curly ever appeared onscreen together. And, believe it or not, it's one of the only two times that Curly ever appeared in a movie with hair! (His second time was in his very last film appearance, *Hold That Lion* (1947), a Columbia Stooges short with Shemp.)

For Stooges fans, seeing a slightly thinner, slightly hairier Curly might seem a little peculiar. Even more peculiar is the plot of *Hollywood on Parade*, a mish-mash comedy revue featuring Jimmy Durante, Rudy Vallee, Ben Turpin, and a handful of bizarre vaudevillians.

This strange assemblage of semi-improvised musical numbers, cast member break-ups, and lame ad-libs somehow seems appropriate for the Stooges' film debut with Curly. As in most of their very early Healy-Stooge films, the boys don't seem to have a handle on what *they're* supposed to be doing, either. Their characters, if you can call them that, are virtually interchangeable. For instance, in this film, Larry gives Moe a slap in the mouth, provoking Moe to belt Curly. Can you imagine Larry giving Moe a crack and getting away with it during the Stooges' heyday?

On the other hand, their routine with Healy—basically a "slapping lesson"—is remarkably well-polished and pretty funny, at least by Stooges standards. Healy's girlfriend, Bonnie Bonnell, appears in the scene with the Stooges, and almost succeeds in ruining it. But after Healy gets her out of the way, it's all Stooges-style slapstick, ending with the machine-gun style "triple slap," seen for the first time on film.

The Stooges appearance in *Hollywood on Parade* is now available on home video in *The Making of the Stooges*, released by Karl-Lorimar Home Video. Retail price is $39.95. If your local video rental store doesn't carry it, you can ask them to order it.

Curly Howard, minus his golden locks.

Although Curly never let Moe get the best of him, he let women walk all over him.

Lost Anecdote #3
"Up in Healy's Penthouse"

Shortly before leaving New York for Los Angeles and *Hollywood on Parade*, Ted Healy called his pal Shemp and his wife Babe and invited them over for a little "bon voyage"-style party at his apartment. Well, before long, Healy had convinced them to join him at the penthouse apartment of a friend, who also happened to be a heroin addict. All too wary and weary of Healy's compulsive pranks, Babe was reluctant, but Shemp convinced her it would be a good time.

Upon arriving at the addict's apartment, Healy convinced his friend to chase Shemp around the balcony, waving a syringe at him supposedly in an attempt to stick him with the needle and "get Shemp high." Shemp was justifiably terrified, running around the balcony trying to avoid the needle. In panicked desperation, Babe threw herself in front of the dope fiend and screamed, "Don't you touch my husband." The addict explained that it was "all in fun," while Healy doubled up with laughter.

The upshot? Shemp said "Nnggg-oaaaah!" to drugs, while Babe Howard said "no" to Shemp's ever rejoining Ted Healy, thus ending an era in Stooge history.

It's obvious from Ted's expression that there was always something going on up in Healy's penthouse. This still is from *Hollywood Hotel* (1937), in which Healy played opposite Ronald Reagan and an all-star cast.

Chapter Three: "Just Think—We Could Have Been Abbott and Costello"

From the first time he saw their act in the 1930s to the very last days of his life, Moe Howard contended that Abbott and Costello regularly stole material from the Three Stooges. He maintained that somehow they were screening the Columbia shorts and that Lou Costello was aping Curly in virtually every film he did. Moe always felt a twinge of frustration whenever he thought about the whole situation—here were Abbott and Costello, making a million dollars a year in features doing *our* stuff, while we were grinding out these cheap little two-reelers and working for peanuts ($20,000 each per year). Moe always wanted the Stooges to star in features, but it took nearly thirty years before they finally clicked into full-length movies, thanks to Moe's son-in-law (and producer) Norman Maurer's tutelage.

However, the Stooges enjoyed *supporting* roles in a number of feature-length films during the 1930s, '40s, and '50s, virtually all of which are "lost episodes," seldom if ever seen on television.

In *Turn Back the Clock* (MGM, 1933), their first film following *Hollywood on Parade*, Moe, Larry, and Curly work together without Ted Healy,

even though technically they were still part of Ted Healy's Stooges. The film, starring Lee Tracy and Mae Clarke, is an engaging comedy-drama similar in concept to both *It's a Wonderful Life* and *Peggy Sue Got Married*. The gist of the story is that Tracy finds out what would have happened if he became rich and powerful and had his life to live over again. Via a dream sequence, Tracy goes back in time to live his life without making any of the "mistakes" he's come to regret. He makes profitable investments and becomes rich. He marries a different woman. He has a completely different lifestyle. In short, he finds out what his life would be like if only he had done things differently. And that's where the Stooges come in.

Tracy finds himself married to a former girlfriend. The Stooges appear at the wedding reception as friends of the groom. Strangely enough, their parts are played quite straight. (The movies' attempt to "reform" the Stooges again?) Moe's hair is slicked back. Larry's is side-parted and raked over his balding dome. Curly's head is still shaven but, with a voice completely free of falsetto, he plays a believable, absolutely normal character named "Ben."

27

The Stooges, rehearsing in civilian clothes and with neatly-combed hair, show their good taste by throwing pillows instead of pies. (Ten bucks to the first fan who can determine what in heck they're supposed to be rehearsing.)

The Stooges' cameo is amazingly softspoken and performed completely without physical comedy.

The boys' major contribution is to get the other wedding guests to join them in an old-fashioned sing-along. With baton in hand, Curly leads a rendition of "By the Light of the Silvery Moon" in three-part harmony.

Curly and Larry seem quite at ease in their straight roles, while Moe appears stiff and a little uncomfortable. Perhaps he was disgusted about the fact that, once again, the Stooges receive absolutely no billing in this, their second feature film appearance.

Despite the slight to the Stooges, the movie is extremely entertaining, and the Stooges' straight cameo is so bizarre, it's a shame that *Turn Back the Clock* has not been released to TV and is not yet available on home video. Will somebody please tell Ted Turner?

The boys had considerably more to do in *Meet the Baron* (MGM, 1933), and it's killer stuff all the way. The cast includes Jack Pearl, Jimmy Durante, ZaSu Pitts, and Ted Healy and His Stooges (now billed as Moe Howard, Jerry Howard, and Larry Fine). The madcap plot of this feature has the shipwrecked Pearl and Durante being rescued in the African jungle after they're mistaken for the legendary lost explorer Baron Munchausen (Pearl's radio character) and his assistant.

Returning home to a tickertape parade, Pearl and Durante are then taken for a stay at Cuddle College, where they meet the campus custodians—yeah, you guessed it, Healy and the Stooges. The boys make their entrance rowing a boat through a flooded basement as they fish for something to give the Baron once he arrives. The entire scene is performed in musical rhyme with the boys trading lines with boss Healy.

In what is the most surprising scene in the film, dozens of female students perform a literal striptease and climb one by one into a community shower. Strangely enough, this stuff gets pretty risque, especially when you consider that this film was produced in the early 1930s. By the time the gorgeous co-eds are well into a song-and-dance number, the water suddenly shuts off, leaving them covered only with soap. Enter Ted and the Stooges.

Initially, though, the boys want no part of repair work—they're in the middle of a card game in the cellar with Healy. But when the cranky Dean of Women/Shower Matron tells them they've got to repair the plumbing before these poor naked girls catch cold, the Stooges make a mad scramble for their tools. And thus we are treated to, (or subjected to, depending on your point of view) that old Stooges chestnut, "What tools?," to which Healy replies, "The tools we've been using for the past ten years!," followed by the obligatory slap.

Once the boys begin working on the pipes, it's classic knockabout farce. The premise of this sequence has Ted and the Stooges blindfolded so as not to embarrass the girls, with the expected confusion and slapstick. The scene is jam-packed with visual gags, bawdy humor, and double entendre, all of which will surely be a treat for the average Stooges fan who might not be familiar with burlesque-style humor.

Regardless of whether you're a hardcore or just appreciative Stooges follower, you'll really get a kick out of seeing the trio perform with the intensely high level of energy they maintain throughout the film. And if wild and violent slapstick is your bag, then Meet the Baron is definitely your movie. There's plenty of choreographed mayhem between Healy and the Stooges, proving that all four can dish it out as well as take it. It's nothing short of mind-blowing seeing Moe getting slapped senseless. Curly gets in on his share of the action, too, but it's Larry who really stands out. Far from the meek, diffident little mouse of the Columbia short subjects, the MGM Larry is a wild man, slapping and slugging and wrestling with a verve and ferocity that parallels Hulk Hogan . . . or at least Andy Kaufman.

Meet the Baron is only occasionally aired on television. You might try contacting the independent station in your market and inquiring if this film is in one of the movie packages they're

leasing. Sometimes stations lease films that just sit on the shelf and are never aired—especially if the leading star (in this case Jack Pearl) is no longer a "draw." Your local station may already have the right to air this film but may not even be aware the Stooges are in it.

While Meet the Baron casts the Stooges as a bona fide threesome, the boys are split up into separate roles in Dancing Lady (1933), also produced by MGM. The film is packed with stars—Joan Crawford, Clark Gable, Fred Astaire, Franchot Tone, Nelson Eddy, Robert Benchley—as well as Healy and the Stooges. But strangely enough, this is another classic that very seldom turns up on TV, even on the Late-Late-Late Show.

In this one, Crawford plays a down-and-out showgirl trying to hit the big time on Broadway. Early in the film she's given her break by Gable, the director of a big-budget production "uptown." The plot takes the usual twists and turns of a show biz-themed movie, as we find Gable producing and financing the show himself after the original producer shuts it down a week before opening night.

In the comedy department, Healy plays Gable's production assistant and stage manager; Larry is cast as "Harry," the show's piano player and accompanist; and Moe and Curly play a couple of dopey stagehands. Although there's plenty of slapstick throughout, the boys perform as a trio in only one scene. The remainder of their contributions, individually and collectively, are divided into vignettes featuring Moe and Curly—with Moe doing little more than repeatedly beating on his partner—and Healy and Larry discussing musical numbers and preparing the cast for rehearsal.

In their only scene as a threesome, Moe (on crash cymbals) and Curly (on the spoons, of course) accompany Larry on piano during Joan Crawford's audition for the show. According to Healy, they are to "give this girl the brush-off"—and that's exactly what they try to do, rushing or dragging the music while she struggles through her dance solo. But the boys blow the Big Brush because Crawford is really quite good, much to Healy's dismay. So she lands a job in the show and the movie rolls on, and on, and on.

Throughout all this, believe it or not, Larry is the comedy centerpiece of the trio. Curly and

Moe are generally pushed into the background, with Larry moving centerstage as the smart aleck of the group. In fact, Healy seems almost more comfortable playing off Larry than either of the Howard brothers.

In his scenes with Healy, Larry is rather aggressive and extremely improvisational—qualities that very rarely, if ever, surfaced throughout the remainder of his lengthy career with the Stooges.

In fact, all three of the Stooges apparently underwent personality changes once they left Ted Healy and joined Columbia Pictures the following year. Stooge fanatics revere Curly as the wildly inventive, childlike madcap as seen in the Columbia short subjects—yet in the MGM films, there are no inventive "Curly" mannerisms, he employs no high-pitched voice, and, in short, he is very un-Curlylike. In addition, the Moe of MGM is completely interchangeable with his partners; there is no indication whatsoever that he is the de facto "leader" of the group. Sure, he stands around and slaps the other two, but he takes it as often as he dishes it out. So it's obvious that, in the initial concept, the Stooges as characters were little more than three jerks whose sole purpose was to supply Healy with punchlines and get beaten up once in a while.

In many ways, though, the Stooges' stuff with Healy is much funnier than their starring stuff at Columbia, with an emphasis on the verbal rather than the visual. The action is much faster-paced than anything they did without Healy, and we can only presume that this resulted from Ted's indisputed creativity and genuine comedic genius. Healy gets virtually no credit for actually inventing the Three Stooges, and is unjustly ignored in terms of his contributions to comedy in general. Everyone from Bob Hope to Milton Berle has claimed to pattern themselves after Healy—his glibness, his cocky walk, his general smartassedness. After all, remarks that Healy literally improvised on stage—cracks like "take the tempo from my body" and the like—were still part of Moe Howard's repertoire some thirty years later.

The "beauty part" of this whole argument is that Stooge fans can see for themselves just how talented Healy really was through viewing films like *Dancing Lady*. In fact, virtually all the Healy/Stooges footage from that film turns up in two different Mark Gilman, Jr. films, *The Making of the Stooges* (Karl-Lorimar Home Video $39.95), featuring the first part of the "audition" scene, and *The Stoogephile Trivia Movie* (MPI Home Video, $19.95), featuring the second part. You can get *The Stoogephile Trivia Movie* by calling Fusion Video toll-free at 1-800-338-7710 and placing an order with your VISA or MasterCard. Both *Making* and *Stoogephile* are also available in video rental stores.

The boys were back playing it as a team in *Hollywood Party* (MGM, 1934), their first all-star feature, starring Jimmy Durante, Jack Pearl (doing his "Baron" thing again), Laurel and Hardy, and Ted Healy and His Stooges. Although this film very frequently turns up on broadcast TV, it originally included Stooges footage that is very often scissored out because of time constraints. (This, in fact, is frequently the fate of Abbott and Costello and Marx Brothers routines—the local stations hack out the comedy set-pieces but keep out-of-date musical numbers in an attempt to retain the basic plotline of the film.)

The plotline of *Party*, such as it is, deals primarily with the notion that Durante's "Schnarzan" pictures are bombing at the box office because the tigers he wrestles look too sickly and pathetic to be truly dangerous. He decides to throw a giant party to welcome the Baron Munchausen, a lion-broker just arrived from Africa. Durante hopes to purchase some ferocious beasts from the Baron to costar with him in his next "Schnarzan" movie.

Enter the Stooges, playing three obnoxious autograph hounds, as well as Ted Healy, appearing as an acquaintance of the Stooges who just happens to be a photographer. The foursome pester every arriving guest at the Hollywood party, regardless of whether they're a celebrity or a nobody. The Healy/Stooges scene is very brief, and after a few slaps are exchanged, Healy is off to snap more pictures. It is, however, "lost" footage that very seldom turns up on most local stations' presentation of the film.

There is more Stooges stuff in *Hollywood Party*, including a scene in which the Stooges are examined by two professors who compare them to cavemen, but this scene is included in just about every local broadcast of *Hollywood Party*.

While Moe, Larry, and Curly were trying to establish themselves in full-length movies, former Stooge Shemp Howard was already making a name for himself as a feature-film character actor. Here he proves to box office giant James Stewart that life isn't *always* wonderful.

And while the movie is far from a showcase for Healy and the boys, it still has some great scenes, most notably a classic Laurel and Hardy egg-fight with comedienne Lupe Velez. It's really a shame that these old musical comedies are so loaded with dull song-and-dance numbers; to paraphrase Durante, this one's "got a million of 'em."

Hollywood Party is very frequently seen on local TV; if the time slot is over ninety minutes, then the Stooges' appearance with Healy will probably be included. If the time slot is under ninety minutes, forget about setting your VCR. And one last note about *Hollywood Party*: it was originally shot and released in two-strip Technicolor, but television stations invariably air an inferior black-and-white print.

Hollywood Party was the last feature the Stooges made at MGM. That same year, 1934, the Stooges left Ted Healy and took up professional residence at Columbia Pictures, where they began their long-running series of 190 two-reel comedies released over a period of 25

years (1934–1959). During this time, they also occasionally appeared in Columbia feature films, the first of which was *The Captain Hates the Sea* (1934).

This "Grand Hotel At Sea" vehicle casts Curly, Larry, and Moe as a trio of musicians on board a luxury liner full of snobs and snobettes. Moe, with hair parted in the middle, "plays" saxophone; Larry is again at the piano with his hair raked straight back; and bald-as-ever Curly is featured on the drums. In one scene, Curly does a surprisingly good job on the skins as he takes a request from one of the guests. Moe and Larry, on the other hand, merely fake it and match their actions to the musical soundtrack.

In their only other scene, the Stooges take a request for "The Wedding March" from a guest about to announce his engagement. Here Larry delivers his—and, for that matter, the Stooges'—only line as he introduces himself to the guest in a Yiddish dialect. Strangely enough, even though the Stooges have no other dialog and no physical schtick in *The Captain,* they are billed as The Three Stooges in the closing credit roll.

The film almost never airs on television and has not yet been released on home videocassette.

Even though their work in Columbia features was limited in the late 1930s, the Stooges manage to steal the show in Columbia's "B" musical *Time Out for Rhythm* (1941). This film represents what is probably the Stooges' best feature film work after their departure from Ted Healy, and it's a real treat for fans of Curly Howard as well.

Although the Stooges are merely a specialty act worked into the framework of the "backstage" story, their stuff stands out as an excellent example of the trio at its peak without Healy. In fact, one scene in particular is a downright classic of farce, rivaling any of Curly's work in short subjects. It's the original screen version of the Stooges' venerable "Maharraja of Vulgaria" vaudeville routine. It's delightfully funny, in no small part due to the fact that it was shot before Curly suffered the debilitating series of strokes that eventually put him out of commission as a physical comic. Stooges fans accustomed to seeing his lackluster performance in *Three Little Pirates* (1947) will delight to his energy level in this earlier version. And he does some almost unbelievably wild acrobatics that only turned up in the Columbia shorts in diluted form. In short, *Time Out for Rhythm* is one of the best examples of Curly's inventiveness, agility, and energy—making it all the more shameful that practically no Stooges fans have ever seen it!

The Stooges are featured in a number of setpieces that showcase their brand of comedy, including a finale dance number in which Moe and Larry dress as caballeros and Curly dons drag in a pseudo-parody of Carmen Miranda. Curly also proves himself the world's original breakdancer by throwing himself to the floor and running around in a circle on his shoulder as the highlight of the number.

It's stuff like this that makes *Time Out for Rhythm* a terrific showcase for Curly Howard as one of the greatest farce comedians of his day. At last report, this, along with a batch of other Columbia musical comedies, had been leased exclusively to cable television for the next decade. So keep your eyes peeled and check your cable listings, because you never know when this one might be popping up in the middle of the night or on a Saturday afternoon.

As good as the boys were in *Time Out for Rhythm*, Columbia's lost episode *Rockin' in the Rockies* (1945) will probably go down in Stooge history as their most pathetic feature film with Curly. The Stooges are given top billing, despite the fact that, once again, they're not working as a threesome, but oddly, are split up into two different factions: Moe plays it as a single, while Curly and Larry are a comedy "duo." The boys are costarred with the "Hoosier Hotshots," a musical quartet that mixes their county-western sound with an attempt to ape the wild musical farce of the great Spike Jones Orchestra.

With plenty of emphasis on the Hoosier Hotshots, it's clear that *Rockies* was not written with the Three Stooges in mind, not to mention the fact that the boys seldom appear together. Moe once again combs his hair straight back and plays a dead-unfunny character named "Shorty," while Curly and Larry more or less enact their Stooge personalities as a couple of vagrants. Shorty meets "The Two Stooges" when he stumbles into them at a local saloon. Curly and Larry are on the run from the law, and Moe/Shorty quickly sizes up their situation. He blackmails them into becoming his partners. In typical "Moe" fashion, however, he also puts himself directly in charge of their finances.

It's pretty much downhill from there. *Rockin' in the Rockies* is full of cartoonish gags, like a talking, mounted deerhead, a talking horse, and, strangest of all, a bit of business in which Curly, for no apparent reason, finds himself with superhuman strength. In one scene he lifts Larry by his feet far over his head to hang him on a mounted moosehead's antlers . . . also for no apparent reason. All of this super-farcical content is woven into a rather straight plotline dealing with the Hoosier Hotshots' desire to get a break on Broadway. And even though they are "rockin'" in the Rockies instead of in Manhattan, the Broadway element is introduced via the presence of a "big Broadway producer" who happens to be vacationing nearby. Through all of this mishegaas we find the Stooges trying to help out the gang, and not providing many laughs in the doing.

But saddest of all is the fact that Curly is so

Director Ed Bernds (left) working as sound man on Frank Capra's *Lost Horizon* (1937). It would be eight more years before Bernds would direct his first Stooge film.

exhausted-looking he's barely recognizable as a Stooge. Quite literally on the verge of a crippling stroke, he stumbles through his performance in a pitiable and labored manner. Add to that the lack of a dominating character (Moe is almost never paired with Curly) and the presence of unfunny, non-Stooge visual humor, and you have a "lost episode" that should stay that way.

Rockin' in the Rockies has also supposedly been leased exclusively to cable TV for a period extending almost to the year 2000. If you're interested, keep checking your local cable listings, because one of these days it might pop up.

Shortly after the release of *Rockin' in the Rockies*, Curly was forced into retirement after suffering a major stroke on the set of the Stooges' short subject *Half-Wits Holiday* (filmed in 1946). At that point his older brother Shemp rejoined the team at Moe's insistence, and the Stooges continued cranking out two-reel comedies for Columbia. In addition, the team of Moe, Larry, and Shemp also appeared in one feature film, *Gold Raiders*, released by United Artists in 1951.

This lost episode was scripted by veteran comedy writer Elwood Ullman (who worked with the Stooges off and on from 1937 to 1965) and Bill Lively, and directed by Edward Bernds, who also helmed the only sophisticated Stooges comedies (if such a thing is possible). *Gold Raiders* is a typical Western, actually, with plenty of cowboys, drinking, shooting, drinking, horses, drinking, and, atypically, the Three Stooges.

The boys fall into the plotline as traveling salesmen who meet up with a local cowboy (George O'Brien) on their way into a small mining town out West. O'Brien hires them as insurance agents for his new mining insurance firm. The boys are in charge of signing new policyholders and sometimes perform the company physicals on prospective clients themselves—with the anticipated results.

Gold Raiders indulges in the usual amount of good guys vs. bad guys stuff, with the Stooges thrown in as comic relief. There's plenty of punishment as dished out by Moe, but most Stooges fans will be disappointed by the lack of actual Stooge participation in the feature. Director Ed Bernds himself was extremely disappointed with the whole project, stating that the film was literally shot in five days, an unbelievably short amount of time in which to shoot an entire feature picture. A telltale lack of production values, as well as the fact that virtually the entire film was shot with one camera angle per scene, indicates that Bernds was forced to use a lot of shortcuts to get the job done. In spite of Bernds's renowned ability to pull tricks out of the bag and make something out of almost nothing, five days of shooting time for a cowboys-and-Indians-style shoot-'em-up was just too tough a sow's ear. *Gold Raiders* doesn't pan out.

Lost Anecdote #4
"Whoops, Ray's an Indian"

Speaking of cowboys and Indians, Moe Howard maintained an ongoing battle of wits with Columbia prop man Ray Hunt, who happened to be of American Indian descent. Moe and Hunt loved to kid each other, and according to director Ed Bernds, sometimes the kidding could get pretty down-and-dirty.

"Ray would suggest a certain prop," says Bernds, "like a breakaway chair to be smashed over the Stooges' heads. And Moe would kiddingly accuse Ray of trying to sabotage them.

"Moe would say things like, 'You *bleeping* Indians are all alike. You hate all white men. Why don't you go back to the *bleeping* reservation where you belong?'

"They'd go back and forth, trading insults like that. And believe me, their language could get really salty."

Chapter Four:
"Hey, George! Hey, Bobby!
Woo-Woo-Woo!"

When the Stooges weren't keeping themselves busy at studios like MGM and Columbia doing feature films, they were doing short subjects—and vice versa. And as we've seen, the studios often took it upon themselves to decide just how *many* of the Stooges would be included in their productions. *Soup to Nuts* boasted a total of four. Some films, as we'll see later, used only two. And some of them broke the Stooges up completely, as in MGM's 1934 short, *Roast Beef and Movies*—the first and only film Curly Howard ever made without another Stooge at his side.

Actually, *Roast Beef* will surely be a surprise for any Stooges fan who is interested enough in checking out this extremely rare (no pun intended) two-reeler. In this one—shot in color, believe it or not—Curly is teamed with George Givot and Bobby Callahan for a very short cameo appearance taking place in a movie producer's office.

The scene opens with the trio attempting to sell their already-produced film project to an extremely uptight producer. George Givot is the group's spokesman, hard-selling the movie

mogul: "The population will eat up our work," he screams. Well, forget about the population—the childlike Curly adds that they'd better hurry up, "or I'll eat it up myself." This exchange comes just moments after a very funny scene in which Curly is apparently suffering from tapeworm and devours an entire bowl of goldfish conveniently planted in the producer's plush office.

After reluctantly consenting to sit through a private screening of their film, the producer watches in horror as Callahan slams down three canned reels of film, while Curly announces he's already eaten the fourth! Givot then proceeds to yank the celluloid from Curly's crotch, along with most of his underwear. But sight gags like that are few and far between; in addition, there is virtually no characterization, physical comedy, or group interplay. Curly might as well have eaten *Roast Beef and Movies*, too, because as two-reel comedy goes, it just doesn't cut the mustard. On the other hand, *Roast Beef* does provide the sole example of Curly Howard working without either of his partners, so it is rather intriguing.

Even in the 1970s, the "Stooge Act without Moe and Larry" idea was still being kicked around. This time Curly Joe DeRita tried to start an act called the "New Three Stooges" with pals Mousie Garner (center) and Frank Mitchell.

Interestingly enough, the film has just recently been added to cable superstation WTBS's film library as a result of Turner Broadcasting's acquisition of the MGM movie vaults. WTBS has already begun airing it; if you missed it the first time around, watch your cable TV listings for its next broadcast.

George Givot and his Stooges—Bobby Callahan (far left), who also played the Messenger in *Men in Black* (1934), and Curly Howard, who played . . . well, you know the story.

Curly getting the lowdown on the birds and the bees from George Givot. No wonder he looks confused.

Lost Anecdote #5
"Sing a Song of Wet Pants"

Even when the Stooges were working solo—while Curly was doing *Roast Beef and Movies* and Moe and Larry were off doing their own single work—they still got together and partied on the weekends. In fact, Shemp's widow, Babe Howard, often commented on how tiresome it was to go to the same show business parties, with the same show business people, watching all the husbands get up and "entertain" with the same old routines while their wives sat around and got bored. But on at least one occasion, the course of events went a little differently. . . .

Babe recalled Shemp taking her to a nightclub in Los Angeles where they were joined by Curly, Larry, Moe, and their wives for an evening of drinks, dancing, and entertainment. During the floor show, Curly got good and loaded and discovered he had to urinate. But instead of stepping into the men's room, Curly merely unzipped his fly and relieved himself under the table all over the ballroom floor. The explanation for such bizarre behavior? "He didn't want to miss the floor show," said Babe. Sounds like Curly created his *own* floor show.

Chapter Five:
"The Two Stooges—Now *That* We Can Afford!"

Curly Howard wasn't the only member of the Stooges to work solo in films. As a matter of fact, each of the Stooges—from Moe Howard all the way down to the last "Third Stooge," Joe DeRita—enjoyed lengthy solo careers before and/or after joining the team.

One of the most curious experiments was casting Moe and Curly without Larry in a couple of films at MGM in the early 1930s. The reasoning behind The Two Stooges isn't clear, but one existing theory is that the studio simply had parts available for a pair of comics rather than for a threesome, thus knocking one of the boys—in each case Larry—out of the picture. It certainly wasn't an attempt by MGM to break up the Healy-Stooge triumvirate; it's doubtful that the studio even cared one way or another whom Healy was employing, whether it be Howard, Fine, and Howard, or a later Stooges group known as Ted Healy's Super Stooges. As long as they had Healy working for them, that was all that mattered; in the 1930s he was one of the biggest stars in vaudeville and a much, much bigger draw than anyone who worked for him, in this case Curly, Larry, or Moe.

The fact that Healy was already a major star

was the reason MGM began grooming him for starring roles in his own feature films. He began working solo in a number of prestigious pictures—*Bombshell* (1933) with Jean Harlow and Franchot Tone; *Operator 13* (1934) with Gary Cooper and Marion Davies; and *San Francisco* (1936) with Clark Gable and Spencer Tracy, among many others—in which he was more or less "stooging" for the leading man or lady himself, generally as comic relief. So that left his *own* Stooges with some time on their hands, prompting MGM to find them solo work in feature films and shorts.

The first screen appearance of the Two Stooges was apparently in a feature titled *Broadway to Hollywood* (1933). Noted film critic, author, and historian Leonard Maltin reports that Moe and Curly play clowns in this one, although in their book, *The Three Stooges Scrapbook*, authors Jeff Lenburg, Joan Howard Maurer (Moe's daughter), and Greg Lenburg state that the MGM legal department claims "there is no evidence available in the studio's legal archives to support the claim that Moe and Curly did in fact appear in that film."

However, there *is* photographic evidence im-

If you were met at the depot by guys who looked like this, you'd climb back on the train too. The Two Stooges, Moe and Curly, in the early 1930s.

mediately available to the general public indicating that Moe and Curly appeared without Larry in an MGM short titled *Jailbirds of Paradise* (1934), made shortly before the Stooges' move to Columbia Pictures. Moe and Curly both play escaped convicts in a film written by Al Boasberg, who would later collaborate on some of the Marx Brothers' funniest screen comedy.

Perhaps even more peculiar than this two-Stooge teaming in the early '30s was the resurfacing of this idea in the mid-1950s. But this time around, the Two Stooges consisted of Moe and Larry, who appeared together in four films made shortly after Shemp Howard's death in 1955.

Actually, Shemp himself also appeared in the

films with Moe and Larry, but only through use of old footage. Sound confusing? Well, here's the explanation: Columbia producer Jules White simply rewrote some "Shemp" Stooges scripts to showcase Moe and Larry, and inserted old footage of Shemp at various points throughout the film to make it appear as if he was actually present during filming. In addition, a double for Shemp, played by Columbia supporting player Joe Palma, appeared in some scenes with Moe and Larry, always seen with his back to the camera. So four Columbia short subjects—*Rumpus in the Harem*, *Hot Stuff*, *Scheming Schemers*, and *Commotion on the Ocean* (all released in 1956)—were produced featuring Stooges Moe and Larry, a fake Shemp, and a lot of old footage.

"Stooges . . . can't live with 'em, can't live without 'em." The Two Stooges—this time Moe and Larry—appeared without Shemp Howard in four "Shemp" Stooges shorts in 1956.

Lost Anecdote #6
"Laugh at First Bite"

"Fake Shemp" Joe Palma may have resembled Shemp from behind, but he never managed to get Shemp's loud, gravelly voice down pat. Longtime Stooges supporting player Emil Sitka—who himself appeared in three of the four "fake Shemp" films—fondly recalls the delights of sharing lunch or dinner across the table from the loud-mouthed Stooge.

Apparently Shemp's normal, offscreen laugh was so loud and hearty that he turned heads wherever he went. On one occasion Sitka got Shemp into a laughing jag during a snack at a posh Hollywood eatery. The hapless, helpless Stooge started laughing so hard that virtually everybody in the place turned to see what all the guffawing was about. When they recognized Shemp, just about everybody started laughing too, and soon Shemp found himself surrounded by a roomful of people laughing at *him*. Shemp, perplexed by the sudden attention, looked himself over, turned to Sitka, and asked, "What the hell—did a bird shit on me?"

Chapter Six:
"Lost but Almost Forgotten"

As either of The Two Stooges could have told you, being a member of Ted Healy's act was far from the steadiest, securest source of income. Aside from the fact that these occasional "duo" teamings resulted from Healy's pursuit of solo work, there were also times when Ted himself was just plain unemployed and unable to pay the Stooges their hundred bucks a week. (When he was working in vaudeville, Ted could be taking in as much as $8,500 per week—and that was during the height of the Depression!) So very often the changes in personnel amongst Healy's Stooges resulted from financial, rather than artistic, considerations.

As has been previously mentioned, Moe, Larry, and Shemp left Ted in 1930 to pursue their own career as an independent comedy act. At that point Healy had signed up three other Stooges—Dick Hakins (whom Healy had employed as a Stooge in the early 1920s), Mousie Garner (a pal of Hakins's), and Jack Wolf (Mousie's cousin)—as replacements. These guys worked with Healy in vaudeville, on Broadway, and, individually, in MGM features. Surprisingly enough, this trio, which also went under the title Ted Healy's Super Stooges and The Gentlemaniacs, made its own series of two-reelers at Vitagraph Studios in the 1930s without Ted Healy.

Unfortunately, very little is known about these films other than descriptions of gags and routines employed specifically by the team for these shorts. For instance, Mousie Garner remembers a piece where all three are trying to take a girl's picture with an old-time flash-powder camera, complete with black skirt. Hakins stands under the skirt, while Mousie stands behind Hakins, lifts his long black dustcoat, and stands beneath *it*. The Gentlemaniacs shorts were apparently peppered with this type of farce.

As for the Gentlemaniacs themselves, their appearances were as wild as the Three Stooges', if not greasier, dirtier, and less wholesome-looking. Jack Wolf was the aggressive "leader" figure of the group, complete with a Joe-the-Bartender-style haircut; Dick Hakins was the quiet, subtler, more off-the-wall middleman, sporting an extremely long side part

Ted Healy's Super Stooges. From left, Dick Hakins, Sammy Wolf, and Mousie Garner. Watch their careers go that-a-way.

The Super Stooges now. From left, Mousie Garner, Sammy Wolf, and Dick Hakins.

that hung like wet toilet paper; and Mousie Garner was the unpredictable, spike-haired lunatic who has often been described as "Curly with Shemp's facial expressions and Larry's haircut." Fans of David Letterman may recall seeing Mousie as a guest on Letterman's "Late Night" program in early 1987, where Mousie was wearing his hair wilder and longer than ever.

But the original Gentlemaniacs split up in the late 1930s when Jack Wolf tired of show business. At that point Sammy Glasser, who agreeably changed his last name to Wolf, replaced Mousie's cousin Jack, and the Gentlemaniacs were reborn. At least one film *is* known to exist featuring this post-Three Stooges comedy team, titled *Hit Parade* (1936), also known as *I'll Reach for a Star*.

In this Republic Pictures musical, the Gentlemaniacs provide a rare glimpse of their vaudeville act, complete with a live, on-camera audience reacting to their antics. The real meat of the show is their wacky song and dance numbers. Their originality, timing, and peculiar stage presence are undeniably unique, as they feverishly—and we mean *feverishly*—sing and dance (or stomp and yell, depending on your opinion) to a raucous nonsense song, providing their own doubletalk gibberish for lyrics. And even though these three trained musicians' strong point was their musical comedy, they can definitely punch, poke, and slap with the best of them. *Hit Parade* contains enough hair-pulling, face-slapping, and head-banging—complete with Columbia-style sound effects—to prove that Howard, Fine, and Howard weren't the only ones who could hold their own as violent comics.

The Gentlemaniacs' contribution to *Hit Parade* is seen almost in its entirety in *The Stoogephile Trivia Movie* ($19.95), available from MPI Home Video. If it's not available at your local video rental store, you can ask the store manager to order it, or better yet—order it yourself by calling toll-free 1-800-338-7710 and use your VISA or MasterCard.

Lost Anecdote #7
"I'll Never File Again"

When the Gentlemaniacs began billing themselves as Ted Healy's Three Stooges, Howard, Fine, and Howard filed a lawsuit to prevent the former threesome from using the Stooges moniker. In fact, Babe Howard remembered Moe visiting Shemp's home in the 1930s and telling him about his plans of putting the Gentlemaniacs out of business, or at least stopping them from calling themselves Stooges.

But as *Daily Variety* reported, the two rival acts—the Three Stooges and the Gentlemaniacs—stumbled into each other at a delicatessen off Broadway in 1938, when both were in town doing vaudeville. *Variety*, however, was quick to point out that "no blows were exchanged." Since a total of six Stooges were present, the show biz "bible" apparently assumed that there might be at least a *little* slapping or poking. In the end, the Gentlemaniacs agreed to back off in using the Stooges' well-known title.

Strangely enough, when Mousie wanted permission to start up a brand new Three Stooges act of his own nearly 40 years later, Moe graciously consented. Even stranger is the fact that he didn't even want a piece of the action!

"Moe was great," says Garner. "He was a real pro. And as a performer, there was nobody that could do that bully stuff better than he could."

Mousie's former partner, Dick Hakins, has his own opinion. "I don't know," says Hakins, referring to Moe's serious offstage demeanor, "I always thought he would have made a good shoe salesman."

Chapter Seven:
"One-Shot, Two-Strip,
Three-Stooge Comedies"

In the mid-1930s, the Gentlemaniacs embarked on a music hall tour of Europe that climaxed with a headliner performance at the Palladium in London. In the meantime, Healy began looking for Stooges again, and Moe, Larry, and Curly ended up signing a new contract with Healy. The foursome began starring in a series of one-shot, low-budget shorts for MGM—all of which quickly became "lost episodes."

The first of these, *Nertsery Rhymes* (1933), is a pretty good example of what the Healy-Stooges vaudeville act with Curly Howard was really like. This short, filmed in two-strip Technicolor, finds the Stooges performing some very familiar routines—virtually all of which they would repeat frequently in their stage and screen appearances over the next twenty years.

The story opens with the makeup-caked Stooges, playing three fairly mature-looking children, snoring sound asleep in a great big bed. Their "father," Ted Healy, is about to leave the room with his lady friend and off-screen girl Bonnie Bonnell, when Curly wakes up demanding a bedtime story. Loving father that he is,

Healy smacks Curly on the noggin. This awakens Moe and Larry, and all three Stooges jump out of the sack to engage in an extremely fast-paced slapstick drill, slipping and sliding effortlessly across the floor in their footed pajamas.

Healy then introduces Larry, or "Junior," to Bonnie as his "smartest son." Bonnie, of course, is skeptical, and decides an interrogation is in order. She segues into the "If I gave you a dollar, and your father gave you a dollar . . ." exchange, so familiar to even peripheral Stooges fans that it doesn't need repeating here. When Larry delivers the "You don't know my father" punchline, Healy delivers a swift smack to his dome. The babylike Stooges then break into a marvelously choreographed punch-, poke-, and slap-fest, easily as violent as anything they did during their Columbia years.

In an attempt to restore order, Moe decides to recite a poem. Moving centerstage, he performs, "Little Fly Upon the Wall," affecting an extremely vaudevillian "effeminate" attitude. When no one reacts, Curly gives it a whirl himself, only to be stopped cold by a disgusted Healy, who threatens to gouge his tonsils out.

Happy-go-lucky Healy waits
for that one "big idea."

Finally, Larry takes a swipe at it: "Little fly upon the track, the train came along and broke his back, woo-woo!" At this point, the Stooges form a human train and scuffle around the room like a locomotive while Larry blows smoke from the back of his pajamas! Grown men playing the Three Stooges playing babies—it's truly as frightening as it sounds. Nertsery Rhymes is undoubtedly the weirdest Healy-Stooge film of them all—and that's saying a *lot*. Certainly well worth checking out, especially for the hardcore Stooges fan who is just dying to see what the boys looked like in color, not to mention Macho Moe playing it "pansy."

Nertsery Rhymes may have approached a level of physical comedy as seen in the Stooges' Columbia shorts, but no MGM film captured the mood, pacing, or use of slapstick of a Columbia film better than Beer and Pretzels (1933).

Pretzels was one of Moe Howard's favorites, and it's definitely the wildest of the Healy-Stooges films as well. This entry finds Ted and the Stooges as unemployed actors who degrade themselves into taking jobs as performing waiters in a restaurant. Even though Bonnie Bonnell is supposed to be the main attraction of the restaurant's floor show, it's Healy and the Stooges who quite literally break up the joint. Fans used to seeing thinly disguised stuntmen recruited for the Stooges' more physical stuff will be delighted to find the boys engaging in bona fide, hardcore, violent, acrobatic slapstick in Beer and Pretzels. For instance, there's a scene where the Stooges provoke a riot involving literally all the restaurant patrons. Both Moe and Larry do some hilariously wild falls that will probably take your breath away if you've only been exposed to their more sedate Columbia films. In addition, young Curly is all over the place, doing fast front-drops to the floor and landing flat on his stomach.

But the most fascinating aspect of the film is its decidedly superior production values. The riot scene at the climax of the film isn't your average Columbia pie-throwing melee consisting of close-up after close-up of people getting nailed. In Beer and Pretzels, the entire cast of fifty or more restaurant patrons is in on the action, simultaneously breaking chairs and clobbering each other in a beautiful extended long shot capturing all the action at once.

Beer and Pretzels is highly recommended, and is undoubtedly the funniest of the Healy-Stooges short subjects.

While Moe often cited Beer and Pretzels as a personal favorite, Larry seemed preoccupied with the following Healy-Stooges short, Plane Nuts (1933). He constantly referred to it in interviews as Around the World Backwards, which actually had been the film's working title.

The interesting aspect of this whole project is that we never do see the Stooges going around the world backwards, which explains the change from the film's original working title to the more generic Plane Nuts.

In this one, Healy and the boys do a facsimile of their stage act, showcasing Healy's fine singing voice. In fact, theatrical producer J. J. Schubert had attempted to build Ted into "the next Al Jolson," even to the point of requesting that he lay off the comedy and just stick with vocalizing. Schubert actually began promoting him as a singing sensation, giving him special advertisement and developing a whole act for him in which Healy was to enter the stage wearing top hat and tails and carrying a walking stick. But Healy, of course, was too much the clown to stand for any of that baloney, and when he made his debut as the New Jolson, he kicked his heels up in the air at the beginning of the number and continued to behave like a goofball throughout the remainder of the song! His audience broke into peals of laughter, but Schubert, disgusted, threw up his hands and walked out of his own theatre.

By 1934, it was all too clear that comedy-, song-, and danceman Healy was doing fine with or without his Stooges. The Stooges, in turn, wanted to move on to bigger and better things. By mutual agreement they parted company, but not until after churning out one more MGM short.

Their last two-reeler together, The Big Idea (1934), unfortunately has very little solid Healy material, very little Stooges participation and very few laughs, period. This one casts Ted as a Hollywood screenwriter in search of "the big idea." The Stooges do little more than wander in and out of the story, playing various musical instruments that spray water at Healy as he tries to concentrate. Once again, Healy's real-life girlfriend Bonnie Bonnell is also on hand, whether you like her or not, as well as an act that calls itself the Three Radio Rogues. (We wonder if Moe filed suit against these guys for using the word "Three" in their billing.)

The film lasts about twenty minutes, which is probably fifteen minutes too long, and was released two months after the Stooges had already signed on with Columbia Pictures for their own starring series of short subjects.

Incidentally, in addition to *The Big Idea*, *Plane Nuts*, *Beer and Pretzels*, and *Nertsery Rhymes*, Healy and the Stooges made one other MGM film titled *Hello Pop* (1933). A print of this film supposedly no longer exists, making it a *truly* lost episode. However, the other four MGM Healy-Stooges shorts were recently obtained by WTBS, the Turner Broadcasting superstation, which in 1987 aired them as part of a prime-time special hosted by comedian Joe Piscopo. Al Hardee, head of the WTBS film department, explained that the station presently has no plans of integrating the MGM two-reelers into their Columbia Stooges shorts collection; however, you can bet the Healy-Stooges episodes will pop up again and again over the next few years, since Turner now owns the MGM library lock, stock, and barrel.

Ted Healy loved cooking up trouble for his Stooges, especially Shemp. This photo was taken after the boys left Healy for greener pastures.

Lost Anecdote #8
"Screw You on a Choo Choo"

Ted Healy and the Stooges may have split up in 1934, but the memories lingered long afterward—especially the off-stage ones. In 1981, Shemp's widow Babe Howard remembered a story that took place in the early 1930s, as Healy and the Stooges—Moe, Larry, and Shemp—were traveling via train to a vaudeville engagement in Canada just across the border from New York state.

Now, there was a strict regulation making it illegal to transport liquor or tobacco over the national boundaries without paying a duty tax. Well, as you can probably gather, Ted Healy was the original Merry Prankster. So, just to see Shemp squirm, he planted a carton of cigarettes in his Stooge's suitcase, and then informed the porter that there was a man aboard attempting to smuggle tobacco over the border without paying tax. Shemp got nailed, was accused of trying to transport tobacco without declaring it, and was detained even after the train pulled into its station in Canada for some more shaking-down. Ted had a good laugh at his pal's expense, but Babe didn't take it so gaily.

Said Mrs. Howard: "That Ted was just downright mean. He loved to make people squirm, especially Shemp. He had a cruel sense of humor that really got under my skin."

Chapter Eight: "Okay, but at Least *I* Can Play a Musical Instrument"

Everyone from Ted Healy to latter-day Stooges producer Norman Maurer expressed the opinion that Larry Fine was perhaps the best natural actor of all the Stooges. In fact, in addition to clowning, Larry was also a talented singer, dancer, musician, and master of ceremonies. He was an all-around vaudevillian, making a fairly good living on stage in the early 1920s, working in a musical comedy act with his wife Mabel Haney and her sister Loretta. So when Larry was inducted into the Stooges in 1925, it was because of his natural performing talent and solid show business experience, right?

Wrong.

Larry Fine was hired as one of the Stooges because of his *hair*. When Healy, Moe, and Shemp dropped backstage at the Rainbow Gardens in Chicago, they were introduced to Larry, fresh from a shower, with his wildly frizzy hair springing up like a million slinkies surrounding his slightly bald head.

One look was all it took. Ted offered Larry ninety bucks a week—an even hundred if he'd ditch the fiddle—to become one of the Stooges. The money was good, it sounded like fun, and—hey, what the heck?

Little did Louis Feinberg know that he'd be making a good living getting slapped, poked, and shoved around on a daily basis for the next forty-five years.

But the request that he "ditch the fiddle" was what always stuck in Larry's craw. Even in a newspaper interview some twenty years later, he was *still* complaining about it: "The only thing I regret about the whole thing," Larry moaned, "is they never let me play my fiddle."

Well, that isn't quite true. Larry fiddled around in a handful of Columbia shorts, including *Punch Drunks*, *Disorder in the Court*, *Fiddlers Three*, and others. So every once in a while, he was given the opportunity to remind his fans that he possessed talent independent of Moe and Curly, or Shemp, or Joe, or whomever he was working with at the time.

In fact, according to critic Leonard Maltin, Larry even made a *solo film*! Yes, a Larry Fine movie appearance without Moe or Curly or any of the other Stooges. A film in which both Larry and Ted Healy were featured in the cast. An

MGM feature titled *Stage Mother* (1933), featuring, as Stanley R. Sogg might put it, "a sterling cast including Alice Brady, Maureen O'Sullivan, and Franchot Tone." And, of course, Larry, doing—you guessed it—a show biz character with a Yiddish accent, as in *Dancing Lady* and *The Captain Hates the Sea.* Who knows? Larry might have even had a legitimate shot at a solo career as a character actor if producers kept casting him in ethnic roles instead of envisioning him

Larry was a quick study (that's a newspaper in his hand, not a script), but he was also quick to head for the dressing room when the director yelled, "Cut!"

only as a goofball with a gag haircut. (Funny, you don't look Stoogish.)

It seems, though, if you really want to get a gander at *Stage Mother,* you'll have to drop by Leonard Maltin's house, because the authors can't find it anywhere in release, either on TV or home video. But you never know—it might pop up on the Late-Late-Late Show some night, so keep checking your local TV listings.

Shemp may have been the only performer at Vitaphone Studios who could wear a sombrero *and* a sweater-vest and still look no weirder than usual.

Lost Anecdote #9
"A Gem of a Game"

Of course, it's only a theory that Larry might have made a good solo character performer. He may have been, as director Ed Bernds has put it, too "flakey" to cut it in the movies without Moe Howard to keep him in line.

It's a well-known fact that Larry was more interested in what the Dodgers were doing than what was happening on the set. "To Larry, making movies was just an unpleasant interruption from listening to the ball game," says pal Emil Sitka. "As soon as the director would yell cut, we'd begin discussing the scene—you know, was it all right, what could we do to improve it, and so forth. But Larry? He was already in his dressing room, listening to the radio!"

Larry's all-time favorite pastime was attending sporting events. Sitka remembers accompanying Larry and two of his cronies—one of them Larry's Columbia stand-in, Charlie Cross—to a Dodgers game at the Coliseum in Los Angeles. "I remember the Dodgers were playing the St. Louis Cardinals," says Sitka. "And Stan Musial is playing for the Cards. Well, the game is going along pretty good, and it ends up a tie in the ninth inning. And who should come up to bat but Stan the Man! I stand up, and I'm screaming, 'Come on, Stan, kill 'em! Kill 'em, Stan!' I'm the type that roots for a favorite player rather than for a particular team. Well, Stan *does* kill 'em! Two runs batted in and the Cardinals beat the Dodgers! So, I'm standing up there, still cheering and yelling, and the next thing I know, Larry is walking away with his two cronies—'Come on, let's get the fuck out of here.' That's the way Larry talked. But he didn't do much talking to *me* on that trip home, I can tell you that! I don't think he said *one word* to me. But that was Larry—he was more fanatical about sports, especially boxing and baseball, than he was about making movies."

Chapter Nine: "I Think Shemp Would Make a Better Ted Healy Than Moe, Don't You?"

Larry Fine may have turned in only one solo film performance in his entire career, but Shemp Howard, on the other hand, was the most prolific of all the Stooges in terms of actual appearances. Between 1933 and 1946, Shemp made a total of 86 films without Moe and Larry, as well as *Africa Screams* (1949), an Abbott and Costello feature produced long after Shemp had rejoined the Stooges.

When Shemp originally left the team in 1932, he was immediately signed by Vitaphone Pictures, a New York-based film company, for appearances in a long-running series of short subject comedies.

In his first solo film, *Salt Water Daffy* (1933), Shemp plays an inconsequential role in support of star Jack Haley. But his next film, *In the Dough* (1933), starring Fatty Arbuckle, gives Shemp quite a bit more to do, including some outrageous slapstick and Stooges-style face-slapping. As usual, Shemp is on the receiving end of the punishment, in this case doled out by character actor Lionel Stander, whom fans of TV's "Hart to Hart" will remember as "Max the Butler."

In this one the action takes place in a bakery, where willing Fatty has just landed a job. Shemp and Stander portray a couple of neighbor-hoods trying to scare some protection money out of Fatty's boss. Unable to collect, Shemp and Stander incite a wild dough fight, and eventually resort to planting a bomb in one of Fatty's cakes. When the scheme literally backfires on the two thugs, they seek revenge on Arbuckle by starting a pie-throwing orgy at the bakery, with the expected slapstick results.

And speaking of slapstick, Shemp does a couple of stunts in this one—particularly one in which a slap from Stander sends him flying up in the air and landing flat on his fanny—that are truly acrobatic in nature. Shemp's fans will really enjoy seeing him in a performance so energetic and agile. In fact, Shemp and Stander virtually steal the show; they dominate their scenes with Arbuckle so effectively that the loveable Fatty just seems to blend into the proceedings like a fourth wall.

Shemp may have been funny in *In the Dough*, but he really went off the wall for *Close Relations* (1933), his second Fatty Arbuckle short. This one casts Fatty as Wilbur Wart, a long-lost relative of senile Ezra Wart, a goofy old codger who just happens to be drawing up his new will. Shemp plays cousin Mole, a derelict type from the "wilted" side of the Wart family tree renowned for its rampant insanity.

The solo Stooge makes his entrance wearing a trench coat and train conductor's hat while bouncing across the room on a pogo stick. Moments later he's back wearing snowshoes and throwing confetti on the floor. Shemp continues to wander in and out of the story, topping himself with one bizarre getup after another until the surprise ending when he falls into a well in Ezra's front yard. Again, Shemp is a scream, playing his part with such deadpan sincerity that his stuff far outshines just about any of the wild physical gags employed by Arbuckle.

But Shemp's best stuff was yet to come. His fourth Vitaphone film, a Ben Blue vehicle titled *Here Comes Flossie* (1933), showcases Shemp as a dopey hillbilly who finds himself in a romantic entanglement with a sleazy dame from the big city.

It seems that brothers Hank and Ezree (Paul Everton and Shemp, respectively) have been given some cash from their father to do whatever they please with. Hank decides to send away for a mail-order bride named Flossie, while Shemp plans on investing his dough in a new cow named—you guessed it—Flossie.

The remainder of the short deals with hired hand Ben Blue's confusion over Hank and Ezree's intentions for their respective purchases. Ben takes Flossie the cow up to the guest room, and Flossie the floozie out to the barn so Shemp can *milk her*. Despite its predictability, *Here Comes Flossie* is pretty entertaining, primarily because of Shemp's contributions. He introduces his hep jive-talking bit, featuring his trademark shadow boxing/interpretive dance moves, as well as a shaving routine that he would repeat years later in the Stooges classic *Brideless Groom* (1947).

And speaking of Stooges-style gags, Shemp's *I Scream* (1934) is virtually loaded with them. This Vitaphone short stars the effeminate Gus Shy as a daffy ice cream salesman recruited by an insurance company to halt the street wars going on between two rival mobs, both of whom hold accidental death policies with the firm.

Lionel Stander plays Moran, the leader of one gang, while Shemp plays his right-hand man Trigger. The dim-witted Trigger is assigned to running the mob's tailor-shop front. And when secret agent Shy tries to infiltrate the gangster's headquarters, all hell breaks loose, climaxing with a gigantic ice cream-fight finale.

This landmark episode is believed to be the very first to make use of such venerable sight gags as the finger-in-the-nostril pull, the hand-block to eye-poke defense, and the use of a human being as ramrod to break down a locked door—in this case, though, the man is reduced to midget-size when they're finished with him.

Though there are gags a-plenty, and Shemp and Stander are again very funny, *I Scream* on the whole is more irritating than entertaining. Gus Shy's stale and peculiar performance as the femmy ice cream salesman, or "dairy queen," is a little too much for contemporary audiences to stomach, and frankly, there's just not enough

No, that's not Emil Sitka tweaking Shemp, but it might as well be. You're looking at the very first Stooge nostril-pull in screen history, from *I Scream*.

Shemp and Lionel Stander to go around. Therefore, I *Scream* should be recommended as curiosity-only viewing for Shempaholics.

For the most part, though, Stooges fans who appreciate Shemp should get a kick out of his early Vitaphone footage. What you're seeing is Shemp more than a decade before he rejoined Moe and Larry, and his stuff is as funny in the early '30s as it was in 1946. He adopts a much zanier, much more aggressive personality, and he does some harrowing pratfalls that you weren't seeing him doing in the late 1940s. (Remember, by the time he reteamed with the Stooges, Shemp was already in his early fifties.) In addition to the acrobatic visual gags, Shemp is a visual gag just to *look* at. For those of you who find the length of Shemp's hair grotesquely funny in itself, you're in for a real treat with these films—his locks are so long and stringy they absolutely defy description. He looks like something out of a zany King Arthur's Court. Imagine how bizarre this must have looked to audiences in the early '30s! All that's missing is the characteristic grease slick he sported in the '40s, which supposedly was used in part because he was by that time dyeing his hair and the process made it very starchy, brittle, and hard to get a comb through without some lubrication.

And speaking of Shemp's hair, it was never wilder nor more ridiculous-looking than in the classic *Dizzy and Daffy* (1934), a Vitaphone short starring real-life baseball legends Jerry "Dizzy" Dean and Paul "Daffy" Dean. Shemp essays the role of retired big league pitcher "Lefty" Howard, forced out of the majors because of his failing eyesight. He appears as a guest pitcher at the Deans' farm-team exhibition game, and he really shows his fans a "pitcher what *is* a pitcher."

Wearing Coke-bottle glasses (a la "The Maha"), the Shemper carries on with some of the wildest pratfalls and goofball pitching schtick imaginable. He's so wound-up, loud, and obnoxious throughout—it's pretty obvious he had a ball making this one. There's also plenty of slapping, some eye-poking, and a cavalcade of terrific Shemp ad-libs. And here's some trivia you can use to startle hardcore baseball fans: in the movie version, which character gave the

"He laid a goldenrod this . . ." Wait a minute—that's another story. This is actually a scene from *Dizzy and Daffy*, in which Shemp regales the Dean Brothers with an old baseball anecdote.

Dean brothers their nicknames? That's right, it was Shemp!

Dizzy and Daffy is a true laugh riot of a lost episode from start to finish. It's wonderful to see Shemp given an opportunity to carry the bulk of the comedy alone, and it was obviously this film that helped propel him into his own series of starring shorts for Vitaphone.

The "Shemp Howard Series," as these subsequent comedies became known, are at least as funny as anything the Three Stooges ever did at Columbia, with or without Shemp. His films with sidekick Daphne Pollard are especially good, and are about as clever and entertaining as two-reelers got in those days. Daphne, usually cast as Shemp's wife, is the perfect foil, and they make a pretty believable pair. She doesn't hesitate to slap Shemp around, and she really lets him have it in a couple of episodes. In real life she was a seasoned pro with plenty of comedy-foil experience—you might even remember her as Ollie's wife in Laurel and Hardy's *Our Relations* (1936).

"Here Comes MacBride . . ." and there goes Shemp's credibility when "Musclebound Pete" (Donald MacBride, left) decides to *marry* the solo Stooge in *Serves You Right*.

regarded by many as the Stooges' best-constructed film, was scripted by Lloyd French. French just happened to be the *director* of *A Peach of a Pair*. Most of the other Vitaphone shorts discussed earlier were directed by Raymond McCarey, who also helmed the Stooges' Oscar contender, *Men in Black*, as well as *Three Little Pigskins* (both 1934). Altogether, McCarey directed seven Vitaphone shorts featuring Shemp.

But of all Shemp's solo films in the 1930s, the fastest, funniest of them all is probably *Serves You Right* (1935), again directed by Lloyd French.

A child stand-in comes in "handy" in this scene from *Serves You Right*, in which Shemp's hand is squeezed down to the size of a little kid's.

Stooges fans might also be surprised to discover the solo Shemp Howard in *A Peach of a Pair* (1934) doing Stoogey bits like the old "turkey-stuffing routine" later seen in *An Ache in Every Stake* (1941), Shemp's own *Listen, Judge* (1952), and many other films. *A Peach* is full of deja Stooge and is probably the funniest of the Howard and Pollard comedies as well, with Shemp and Daphne playing a vaudeville act titled "Cook and Butler." Those are their names—Shemp Cook and Daphne Butler—but a society couple mistakes them for the cook and butler they need to prepare dinner for their swanky party. (Sound familiar, Stooges fans?) Shemp and Daphne, meanwhile, think they've been hired for a club date as entertainers. The plot pretty closely follows the same storyline as the Stooges' *Crash Goes the Hash* (1944) with one major exception: Shemp accidentally serves everybody drinks loaded with alum! This bit, of course, later turned up in the Stooges' *No Census, No Feeling* (1940).

It's really no mystery why much of the content of *A Peach of a Pair* turned up in films like *An Ache in Every Stake* and others. For instance, *An Ache,*

Whether it was placekicking or facekicking, Shemp was always more than willing to go "all the way" physically to get a laugh. In his Vitaphone shorts, Shemp does slapstick that would make a stuntman cringe.

Shemp is hilarious as an errand boy for a stuffy law firm, struggling to convince his boss to promote him to fulltime process server. He finally gets his big break when he's called upon to serve a court summons to a big bone-crusher named Musclebound Pete (Donald McBride).

One of Shemp's all-time funniest pieces of improvisation comes when he asks another employee for a few pointers on serving an unwilling defendant. After a particularly aggressive demonstration by his fellow server—in which the guy practically ties Shemp up in his own suitjacket—Shemp tries it out himself, and is soon slipping and sliding all over the floor in his inimitable seizure-like ballet, rehearsing in

pantomime for his big chance to stick Musclebound Pete.

But things don't go quite as smoothly as Shemp had envisioned, and during the course of the film, we watch him endure a series of horrific, cartoon-like tortures that are as funny as they are outrageous. First, he gets his hand literally squeezed down to the size of a baby's. Then he is punched through a wall where he hangs disembodied but with limbs twitching and spasming all around him. Finally, in a desperate move, Shemp dresses as a woman and goes after his prey, knowing that Pete's "afraid of anything in skirts." But this is two-reel comedy, so naturally Pete proposes marriage to the hapless Shemp moments after meeting him/her!

All of this stuff is weird and extremely funny, absolutely establishing Shemp as the funniest of all the Stooges. (We know it sounds like blasphemy, but it's true nevertheless.) The sight gags and pratfalls are innumerable in this action-and-laugh-packed episode, and Shemp's timing is right on the mark in every scene.

This and all of the Vitaphone "Shemp" shorts mentioned in this chapter are available from Channel 13 Video at varying prices. Channel 13's address is P.O. Box 15602, N. Hollywood, CA 91615. You can write them for the details, but make sure you send a self-addressed, stamped envelope.

In addition to the Vitaphone films, Shemp also appeared in two miscellaneous shorts for Van Beuren in 1934: *Henry the Ache* and *Knife of the Party*. Fortunately, both of these films are also available on home video.

Disappointingly, though, Shemp's appearance in *Henry the Ache* is the smallest film role of

The laugh is on Bert Lahr (right). He may have been the star of *Henry the Ache*, which featured Shemp in a tiny bit part, but nobody's asking for a "Bert Lahr's Lost Episodes" book.

his career. Bert Lahr is the headliner as the pompous King of England in this slow-moving two-reeler. The plotline is a parody of Charles Laughton's *The Private Life of Henry VIII*, retaining primarily the element of "wife-trouble."

When Henry decides to have his fourth wife, Queen Ann, hanged, he meets with his faithful assistant "Archie" (Shemp), who is listening to a radio (!) play-by-play of the execution. Once the dirty deed is done, widower Henry announces his intentions of finding a new bride. Shemp steps in as the "Keeper of the Little Black Book," fixing up Henry with wife-to-be Catherine.

The remainder of the short deals with Lahr's inability to please his new spouse, as well as the affair that quickly develops between the queen and a disloyal member of Henry's court. (Stooges fans will recognize Monty Collins, who played the movie director in *Three Missing Links* [1938], as the queen's boyfriend.)

The closing gag of *Henry the Ache* is actually the highlight of the film as the *real* Charles Laughton makes a cameo appearance as the infamous Bluff King Hal. *Henry the Ache* is available on home video in a compilation of oddball Stooges films titled *The Joy of Stooge-ing* (Madhouse Video, $19.95). You can get it by calling Fusion Video toll-free at 1-800-338-7710 and ordering with your VISA or MasterCard.

Shemp had considerably more to do in his other Van Beuren short released by RKO, *Knife of the Party*. In fact, he and four Keystone Cop-types are billed as Shemp Howard and His Stooges—although they posed absolutely no threat to Ted Healy and company.

Although Shemp and pals receive special billing, a comedian named Jack Good stars as the manager of a mediocre vaudeville troupe that employs a ton of showgirls and the five madcap stage comics.

This pathetic vaudeville company is paid their salary in celery as well as other produce and poultry. This paves the way for an extremely peculiar scene in which Shemp and his idiots attempt to cut a coconut with a lumberjack's saw. When it's obvious that these "Stooges" are getting nowhere fast, Shemp steps in and delivers filmdom's first (and perhaps only) "quadruple slap." He then takes

This compilation includes offbeat Stooges footage, ranging from an animated Curly to Moe doing a sit-down, stand-up routine.

charge of the proceedings and instructs the boys to open the fruit Stooges-style—by "using their heads."

The action gets sillier from here on out, as the group finds itself paying off its enormous hotel bill by performing menial jobs around the building. Weirdness prevails as Shemp leads a Revolutionary War-style truckin'-and-jivin' brigade through the hotel lobby, eventually finding himself in the midst of an outrageously wild and decidedly unfunny floor-mopping free-for-all with his Stooges.

But despite the overblown goofiness, Shemp

fans will undoubtedly get a charge out of his indoor golfing routine, his inventive food-swiping scheme, and a pre-dinner football game with a roast beef featuring Shemp as quarterback. Even though Shemp handles himself with aplomb as leader of the gang, his cronies don't demonstrate any individual comedic characteristics of their own. One wishes Knife of the Party had a lot more Shemp and a lot less of his four "Stooges."

But decide for yourself—Knife of the Party is also available in its entirety in The Joy of Stooge-ing.

Lost Anecdote #10
"Stooling Around"

Stooges director Ed Bernds considers Shemp to be his favorite of all "Third Stooges"—and Bernds worked with Curly and Joe DeRita as well as The Greasy One. Ed recalls with a laugh the story sessions he used to conduct with the Stooges at Columbia, where Moe, Larry, and Shemp would contribute ideas for their next two-reel comedy.

"When we had a story conference, the Stooges would reminisce, and kick around old ideas, but no matter what happened, Shemp always managed to segue into the story of the bear that moved its bowels on stage. I guess the Stooges were working in vaudeville with a trained bear, and on one occasion, the bear just unloaded himself in the middle of their act. And Shemp loved that story. By the end of it he'd be laughing out loud, extending his arms and saying, "He laid a goldenrod this long!"

Chapter Ten:
"Say, Shemp . . . Let's Hear Your N'Yuk-N'Yuk-N'Yuk!"

When his Vitaphone contract expired in the late 1930s, Shemp moved from New York to California and purchased a home right down the street from Moe, as well as Jules White, then head of Columbia Pictures' short subject division. Shemp and Babe Howard became chummy with Jules, who eventually set Shemp up in his own series of two-reelers at Columbia.

"Shemp got the work because Jules was a friend of the family," said Babe Howard. "The Stooges were already working for Jules, and he managed to get Shemp his own series, too. I think in the long run it was pressure from both Moe and Jules that convinced Shemp to take Curly's place when Curly got sick."

But before rejoining the Three Stooges, Shemp made five starring two-reelers under White's direction, all released between 1944 and 1946. In all of these films, director White requested that Shemp "do" brother Curly Howard—Jules loved Curly's work and apparently tried to turn every slapstick comedian he knew into an approximation of the shaven-headed clown.

"Instead of letting the actors do it their own way, Jules would ask the actors to ape his actions," says Ed Bernds. "I can remember watching Jules direct Shemp and demonstrating how he wanted something done. And he would stand up there and do takes, and that kind of thing, and Shemp would just cringe! No actor wants to imitate someone else, and Shemp, especially, hated that kind of thing. Jules, of course, wanted Shemp to be Curly. But Shemp had his own way of doing things, which, to my estimation, was a very good way. He could never be Curly; that just wasn't his style."

As Jules himself put it, "Shemp was very, very good—but he wasn't quite Curly."

But Bernds allowed Shemp to do his own thing in the four solo shorts they collaborated on. In fact, the Shemp of Columbia's "Shemp Howard Series," directed by Bernds, is generally offensive, bombastic, and obnoxious—just the way Stooges fans like him.

The first Bernds-Shemp collaboration, *Where the Pest Begins* (1945), was written by Bernds and directed by Harry Edwards. This one finds married couple Tom Kennedy and Christine

McIntyre moving in next door to the neighborhood jerk (guess who?). As soon as Shemp meets the beautiful Christine, he introduces his own wife (Rebel Randall) as "my mother-in-law's daughter." Shemp decides to help his new neighbors move in, and in the process crushes Kennedy's foot, smashes his chin, brains the poor slob with a sledgehammer, and drives Kennedy's car through his garage door.

But that's just for openers. A typical wartime production, the film miscasts Kennedy as a government-contracted explosives expert who leaves live bombs lying around the yard. Shemp accidentally hurls one through the air, and they both take cover on the ground. But much to Kennedy's disappointment (and Shemp's delight), the bomb turns out to be a dud, landing with nothing more than a quiet puff of smoke.

By now, Kennedy is beside himself. One afternoon with Shemp has practically driven him to the edge of a nervous breakdown. Shemp tries to calm him down and offers him a swig of his home brew—"Shemp's Special."

The boys mix a drink for Vernon Dent (reclining on couch). Come to think of it, if the Three Stooges were mixing you a drink, it might be more prudent to recline *under* the couch. From "The Frank Sinatra Show."

With one gulp, it's fire and smoke out of Kennedy's ears. Of course, all's well that ends well when Kennedy realizes that one jigger of "Shemp's Special" is all he needs to turn a bomb of a bomb into a big bang.

Where the Pest Begins is a weak, confusing episode suffering from erratic direction and bizarre casting. Tom Kennedy is neither a funny counterpart nor an adequate straight man to Shemp's aggravating antics. Add to this some very distracting reaction shots peppered throughout the film, and what you have is a gag-laden script with plenty of promise that never goes anywhere.

On the other hand, Bernds's first directorial effort with Shemp, *Mr. Noisy* (1946), has some hilarious moments and is a pretty good representation of the obnoxious "Shemp" character at its best. The script, a remake of and improvement on Charley Chase's *The Heckler* (1940), showcases Shemp's infamous loud mouth. He plays a habitually overbearing heckler at various sporting events, and Shemp's fans will delight to his nonstop ad-libbing and scenery-chewing. What the film lacks in flow, continuity, and logic is more than made up for by Shemp's mischievous behavior and raw comedic talent.

The film opens with Shemp screaming and jeering his way through a national tennis match, followed by two World Series games. He manages to infuriate both spectators and athletes, and it's belly laughs all way. At one World Series game, Shemp tosses tobacco tins, peanuts, burning matches, and sizzling insults at everyone who happens to be unlucky enough to be seated around him. At one point he even shakes up a bottle of beer, sprays it at the crowd (which includes Stooges veteran Vernon Dent), and yells, "Don't call the game! It's only a *shower*! Get it?" followed by that ridiculously loud and ear-piercing Shemp Howard laugh.

After one of his tirades results in a player blowing the second-to-last game of the series, Shemp is recruited by a couple of gambling thugs to help them fix the final game. Shemp obliges, and begins tormenting the "losing" team in their locker room the very next day. Knowing what Shemp has in store for them, they, too, employ a couple of thugs on their own to take care of Mr. Noisy before he gets a

Shemp drops in on bellboy Billy Benedict ("Whitey" from the Bowery Boys films). It was at poverty-row Monogram that Shemp costarred in three feature films.

chance to screw up the final game. They sneak into Shemp's hotel room while he's sleeping and cover him with ice, hoping he'll catch pneumonia. Shemp does a great talking-in-his-sleep bit as the thugs load him up with cubes. But when Shemp wakes up the next morning with a hoarse voice, his comrades rush him to the doctor for an emergency pre-game physical.

One of the best bits in Mr. Noisy comes when the doctor swabs out Shemp's throat with a three-foot cotton-swab-on-a-stick. Inevitably, the cotton ball falls off while the doctor is ramming the instrument in and out of Shemp's esophagus. With the cotton ball lodged in his throat, Shemp is unable to heckle anymore because his voice sounds like Baby Snooks.

Even though the plot is somewhat confusing, the surprise ending is very funny and the short moves along at a fast pace. Loud and clear, Mr. Noisy is a gem of a lost episode—especially for diehard Shemp fans.

Shemp abandons the "pushy" character in favor of his more Stoogelike "diffident" persona in his final solo short, Bride and Gloom (1947). The

Larry's constant eating during production seems to tickle Curly Joe to no end.

film was again directed by Ed Bernds, and features a supporting cast consisting of Stooges veterans Jean Willes, Christine McIntyre, Dick Curtis, Vernon Dent, Emil Sitka, and Heinie Conklin, among others. This one draws from the basic plotline of Charley Chase's silent film, *Limousine Love* (1927), concerning the misadventures of a poor sap late for his own wedding.

We find Shemp on his way to the church, where bride-to-be Jean Willes and her father, Vernon Dent, are waiting with assorted family members for Shemp's arrival. Problem is, Shemp's car is in the shop and he has to take a cab. But when cab driver Emil Sitka gets his vehicle stuck in a deep mudhole, Shemp is forced to borrow his own car back from the mechanic—without knowing the car has no brakes!

After slamming into a fireplug and drenching a beautiful passerby (Christine McIntyre), Shemp, always the gentleman, is forced to give the soaking-wet girl a ride home. Of course, her place is located directly across the street from the church where they're waiting for Shemp! Unable to stop the car—remember, even if he *had* brakes, he doesn't want his fiancee and her family to see what he's got in the backseat— Shemp just keeps circling around the block, waving merrily. Finally, Shemp is caught trying to sneak the disrobed Christine out of his car, with the expected results: the wedding is called off, Shemp gets arrested by the police for reckless driving, and, as an added bonus, Christine's husband Dick Curtis shows up and punches Shemp in the nose.

Eventually Shemp gets the whole mess straightened out, and he winds up marrying Jean after all. However, Shemp keeps running into Christine and her psychotically jealous husband, who just happens to be a prizefighter. The remainder of this episode is essentially bedroom farce, with Shemp doing everything he can to avoid running into Curtis. As this kind of thing goes, it's not bad, and there are a lot of very funny touches, such as a scene in which Willes tells Vernon Dent she couldn't possibly live without Shemp. "He's so-o-o beautiful," she sighs. Dent wrinkles his face in distaste as the audience gets a look at Shemp's picture, obviously indicating that he's so-o-o homely.

Unfortunately, the Columbia "Shemp Howard Series" episodes are not in general release to TV or home video.

As Jules White himself put it in an interview shortly before his death, "There's a tremendous amount of material there above and beyond the Three Stooges, and I don't have any idea why Columbia doesn't put it out."

If you want to see for yourself, our suggeston is to contact the Three Stooges Fan Club— someone there might be able to give you a lead on where you can get your hands on the films.

Lost Anecdote #11
"I Can Hardly Drive"

During the shooting of *Bride and Gloom*, director Ed Bernds asked Shemp to drive a car in and out of camera range for a specific shot. Shemp, who was usually very cooperative, refused.

"I guess he was scared to death of driving," says Bernds. "He had never learned how to drive, and he was so afraid of cars that he literally would not get behind the wheel of a car in ignition."

So Bernds explained to Shemp that he really wouldn't have to *drive* the car—all he'd have to do would be to step on the brake once he was out of range. *Still* no go. Then Bernds suggested that they simply put the car in neutral and have a couple of stagehands *push* Shemp out of frame, at which point Shemp would then step on the brake.

Sorry, still no go. Shemp refused even to touch the *brake!*

What Bernds finally wound up doing was quite elaborate for such a simple shot. He assigned a couple of stagehands to push Shemp's car into frame; as soon as he was out of camera range, they stopped the car by pulling on it with a rope that was tied to the back bumper!

Chapter Eleven: "A Shemp Stooge Act? Wait a Minute, This Sounds Familiar . . ."

In addition to the shorts for Vitaphone and Columbia, Shemp also costarred in a trio of feature-length comedies at Monogram: *Three of a Kind* (also known as *Cookin' Up Trouble*), *Crazy Knights* (also known as *Ghost Crazy*), and *Trouble Chasers* (also known as *Here Comes Trouble*). Each film was shot in 1944 on an assembly-line basis and was strictly bottom-of-the-bill fare. In these low-budget quickies, Shemp was part of a Stooges-type ensemble with real-life pals Billy Gilbert and ex-boxer Maxie Rosenbloom (both of whom Shemp eventually went into business with). Shemp and Gilbert once co-owned—get this—a chicken farm, while Shemp and Rosenbloom started a restaurant together. Both endeavors failed miserably. However, when the trio put their heads together for a feature film, the results were always moderately entertaining, with *Three of a Kind* standing out in particular.

The plotline of *Three of a Kind* deals with everything from the death of vaudeville to child-custody regulations. Billy Gilbert is the real star of this one, which follows the wacky adventures of an unemployed acrobatic team

called "Gilbert and Howard." Not only do Billy and Shemp find themselves out of work, but they also wind up playing nursemaid to the whiney son of a fellow acrobat who died in a fall on stage.

Gilbert and Shemp perform as a duo throughout most of *Three of a Kind*, enacting a number of set-pieces in which we find them appearing on a radio quiz show, cleaning windows, dressing mannequins, and washing dishes. But the real fun starts when Maxie Rosenbloom—who actually has very little to do in this entry—hires the boys as cooks for his cafe. Shemp and Billy manage to pull off some really wild ad-libbed exchanges while they attempt to maintain order in Maxie's kitchen.

And as visual gags go, most of them are pretty Stoogey. For example, in the process of making a huge pot of soup, Shemp adds about a half can of paint, much to Billy's horror. Shemp then attempts to rectify the situation by adding a couple of quarts of paint remover, much to Billy's approval, of course.

Though the boys perform a weird little vaudeville-style floor show at the restaurant, most of

Shemp was once named the "ugliest man in Holly-wood," and real-life pal Billy Gilbert (far left) seems to be noticing it for the first time. From *Three of a Kind*.

their interplay is restricted to verbal comedy. There is minimal slapping and slugging, and most of it is dished out by Gilbert with Shemp as the slapee. In fact, Shemp looks as if he's just been slapped around throughout most of the movie; he's tired-looking and there is very little spark in his performance, with the exception of his beloved improvisational sequences with Gilbert.

Fans expecting a different set of Three Stooges will be greatly disappointed with all of these Monogram features. However, if you're a Shemp freak, you might get a kick out of his ad-libbed stuff with Billy Gilbert.

At least he *looks* the part, which is more than can be said of Billy Gilbert. From *Three of a Kind*.

Shemp as a fight trainer for Slapsy Maxie Rosenbloom?

All three of these features have been licensed to television in local markets, but they infrequently, if ever, turn up on the air. (In fact, product from Monogram seldom is run unless it features name stars like Bela Lugosi or the Bowery Boys.) You might contact your local independent TV station—try starting with whichever one seems to be playing a lot of old junk—and ask if they have these films in their libraries. If they do, you might be able to persuade them to throw a Gilbert-Howard-Rosenbloom on the air at three o'clock in the morning instead of some bad western or monster movie.

Lost Anecdote #12
"Fields Blows His Top"

In addition to his costarring films with Billy Gilbert and Maxie Rosenbloom, Shemp Howard made appearances in a total of 38 feature-length movies betwen 1935 and 1949. His most famous feature film work was undoubtedly in *The Bank Dick* (1940), considered by many critics to be W. C. Fields's masterpiece of comedy.

Fields wrote a fairly large supporting role for Shemp as Joe Guelpe, the bartender. But, despite the fact that Shemp receives billing toward the top of the cast list, he has very little to do in the film. And that's because poor Shemp was literally too funny for his own good!

"Shemp had a very poor opinion of W. C. Fields," says Emil Sitka. "Any time his name was mentioned, Shemp would say, 'That son-of-a-bitch Fields cut out my best stuff!' He was really unhappy about that. But that was the way things worked in those days. The star was the boss. And if Fields didn't want it in there, it got cut out!"

During shooting, Fields had personally taken Shemp aside and instructed him to lay off the funny stuff. Shemp ignored him, did his thing, ad-libbed like crazy, and all of his priceless improvisation was subsequently captured on film. But Fields saw to it that most of it wound up on the cutting-room floor.

And Sitka should know—he frequently fell victim to the reality of the Hollywood power structure. For example, Sitka had played the role of a persnickety garbage collector in *The Good Humor Man* (1951), starring Jack Carson. The director loved Emil's nuances, moves, and ad-libbed business. Jack Carson thought they were funny, too—way *too* funny. The next thing Emil knew, he was being asked to come back to reshoot his scene.

"I asked the director, was there something wrong?" remembers Sitka. 'No,' the director said, 'just come back and do it again, please!' Well, I did. And when I finally saw the finished version on the screen, practically the entire scene consisted not of me *doing* the business, but of a reaction shot of Jack Carson *watching* me doing the business."

Even today, the gracious genius Sitka has kinder words for Jack Carson than Shemp had for the legendary Mr. Fields.

Chapter Twelve: "Whatta Ya Mean, Bad Taste? This Stuff'll Wow 'Em!"

Nowadays, you can get away with just about anything in the movies. (We wonder, though, if the forthcoming made-for-TV Stooges biography will include anything like Shemp calling W. C. Fields a son-of-a-bitch.) Surprisingly enough, the Three Stooges apparently got away with some stuff back in the 1930s and '40s that they couldn't get away with when their films hit TV in the late '50s.

What we're referring to here is lost *footage* from the Stooges' Columbia short subject series. Stuff that was cut out more than a quarter century ago and is just now resurfacing through the release of the Stooges' shorts on home video. Material that originally played on theater screens but has been kept buried by Columbia Pictures ever since.

The first deletion on record is the soul-kiss gag from *Movie Maniacs* (1936). Moe, playing a would-be director, demonstrates how to give a screen kiss, and winds up being bent over backwards by a pretty starlet, who more or less takes control of the situation. That gag is one of many that has been restored by Columbia Pictures for the home video release of that film.

We don't know if it was scissored out because it was sexy or because somebody thought it was in bad taste. As far as bad taste goes, there are Stooges gags that would definitely fall into that category, at least from the viewpoint of a scissor-happy editor trying to make the Stooges' films more palatable for television's kiddie audiences.

For example, *Three Sappy People* (1939) presents a sight gag involving a man wearing a wooden leg with a sign on it reading "Post No Bills." *From Nurse to Worse* (1940) includes the line, "Take these bodies to the crematory." *So Long, Mr. Chumps* (1941) has Curly making a crack about "hanging out at the gallows." There are probably lots of other gags that we're not even aware of that were pulled when Columbia released the films to TV. We haven't seen the completely uncut, unedited prints of the original films.

And, in addition to "bad taste" remarks, there are the racial slurs. And really cruel ones at that. Slams at the Japanese in *Sock-A-Bye Baby* (1942) and *Three Loan Wolves* (1946), for example. Strangely enough, Columbia chose to

Huntz Hall, a protege and mega-fan of Shemp's, proves he *is* fit to tie the laces of Shemp's boot in these family snapshots taken in 1942 on the set of *Private Buckaroo*.

leave that stuff intact when the films went to TV—they were apparently more worried about dumping the word "crematory" than the no-holds-barred remarks about "the enemy" more than a decade after World War II. Very seldom, though, do these anti-Japanese remarks turn up on local airings of the Stooges; the TV stations themselves generally do the editing, not Columbia.

All of this stuff—whether it's "bad taste" gags or offensive racial content—turns up intact in the home video versions of these old films. And in pristine prints, too, actually taken from the original 35-millimeter negatives. The films are released at varying prices by Columbia Pictures Home Entertainment (three episodes per tape), and, if your local video store doesn't already carry them, you can request that they do.

Lost Anecdote #13
"Stooge in Arms"

The Stooges may have indulged in the occasional bad-taste joke, but to Shemp Howard, just asking him to work with animals was in *itself* a bad-taste joke.

Shemp, you see, was scared to death of most animals. Babe Howard says he used to carry a big stick with him as a weapon whenever he took a walk around the neighborhood after dark. That was in case he had to fend off some vicious dog, or, perhaps, a rabid cat or squirrel. Actually, Shemp was rather fond of animals—as long as he didn't have to get near them.

Shemp maintained that cautious attitude when it came to his screen appearances as well. During the research of this book, the authors stumbled upon a Hal Roach-produced feature film from 1940 titled *Road Show* that includes a brief appearance by Shemp as a *lion*-keeper! (This film has not previously turned up in official Shemp Howard filmographies, probably because his name does not appear in the movie's credits and, therefore, probably not in any official records, either.)

In the storyline, Shemp plays a character named "Moe" (yeah, we know it's confusing) who sells a ferocious lion to a traveling carnival, or "road show." But the former Stooge doesn't get near any real lion in the film—the closest he gets is in a shot in which he appears to be looking at the beast through the bars of its cage.

And that's about it for Shemp's contribution to *Road Show*, which stars the ever-dapper Adolphe Menjou along with veteran comics Patsy Kelly (former stooge to vaudevillian Frank Fay) and Willie Best (better known as "Sleep 'n' Eat") in support. The movie is typical, predictable fare which probably ran on the lower half of a double bill. There are plenty of bizarre plot twists, plenty of musical interludes, but, obviously, very little Shemp—about four lines of dialogue in all. What's more, he plays his part completely straight, and, unless you were in the know, you'd never guess he was a former vaudeville Stooge.

Chapter Thirteen: "Record the Stooges Vaudeville Act? I Think It's a Waste of Film, but . . ."

Some Stooges lost episodes are *really* tough to dig up, especially if their very existence is not a matter of public record. Case in point: the Three Stooges' home movies!

In the 1930s and '40s, Moe Howard owned a 16-millimeter camera and projector setup for making and watching his own home movies. Stoogemaniacs were stunned when, in 1982, Joan Howard Maurer appeared on NBC's "Late Night with David Letterman" and brought along some black-and-white home movies of the Stooges and their families from the 1930s. The bulk of the footage dealt with Curly's wedding to second wife Elaine Ackerman in 1937, with Moe, Larry, and Shemp clowning for the camera.

In addition, there also exists *color* home movie footage of the Stooges shooting *Back from the Front* (1943), a Columbia short subject, filmed by a friend of the Stooges' family, Judge Brand.

Where can you get your hands on this stuff? Well, the first batch of films—with Moe, Larry, and Shemp joining Curly at his wedding—have been aired not only on "Late Night," but also were rebroadcast as part of "Hollywood Home

Movies" the following year, hosted by Bill Cosby. Someone in the Three Stooges Fan Club probably has one of those shows on tape.

On the other hand, there is existing footage of the Stooges' *vaudeville* act that is not only still around, but also is commercially available through various sources.

In *The Making of the Stooges*, scenes from their stage act with Curly filmed at Chicago's Oriental Theatre in 1942 turn up about midway through the program. We see the boys doing a routine where Curly, as usual, is on the receiving end of a lot of slapping. In addition, we are treated to a live stage version of him doing what was later nicknamed "The Curly Shuffle," plus a shot of him spinning around in a circle on the floor, amongst other bits of business.

Making of the Stooges also includes footage of the Stooges' stage act twenty-five years later—shot in color and featuring Joe DeRita—taken by a fan during an outdoor personal appearance at a fair in Dallas.

Plus—as a special bonus—the hour-long documentary also includes footage of the Stooges hamming it up at a celebrity charity baseball game, with Curly raising hell in the dugout and barking at the camera. This piece was lifted from a Ken Murray home movie filmed in the 1940s.

In addition to *Making Of*, a follow-up film, *The Stoogephile Trivia Movie*, also features footage from the Oriental Theatre that didn't turn up in the first compilation. In fact, there is considerably more home movie content in *The Stoogephile*, giving the curious fan a better opportunity to see Moe yanking both Curly and Larry around, as well as the customary slapping and smacking. The 16-millimeter footage turns up at the

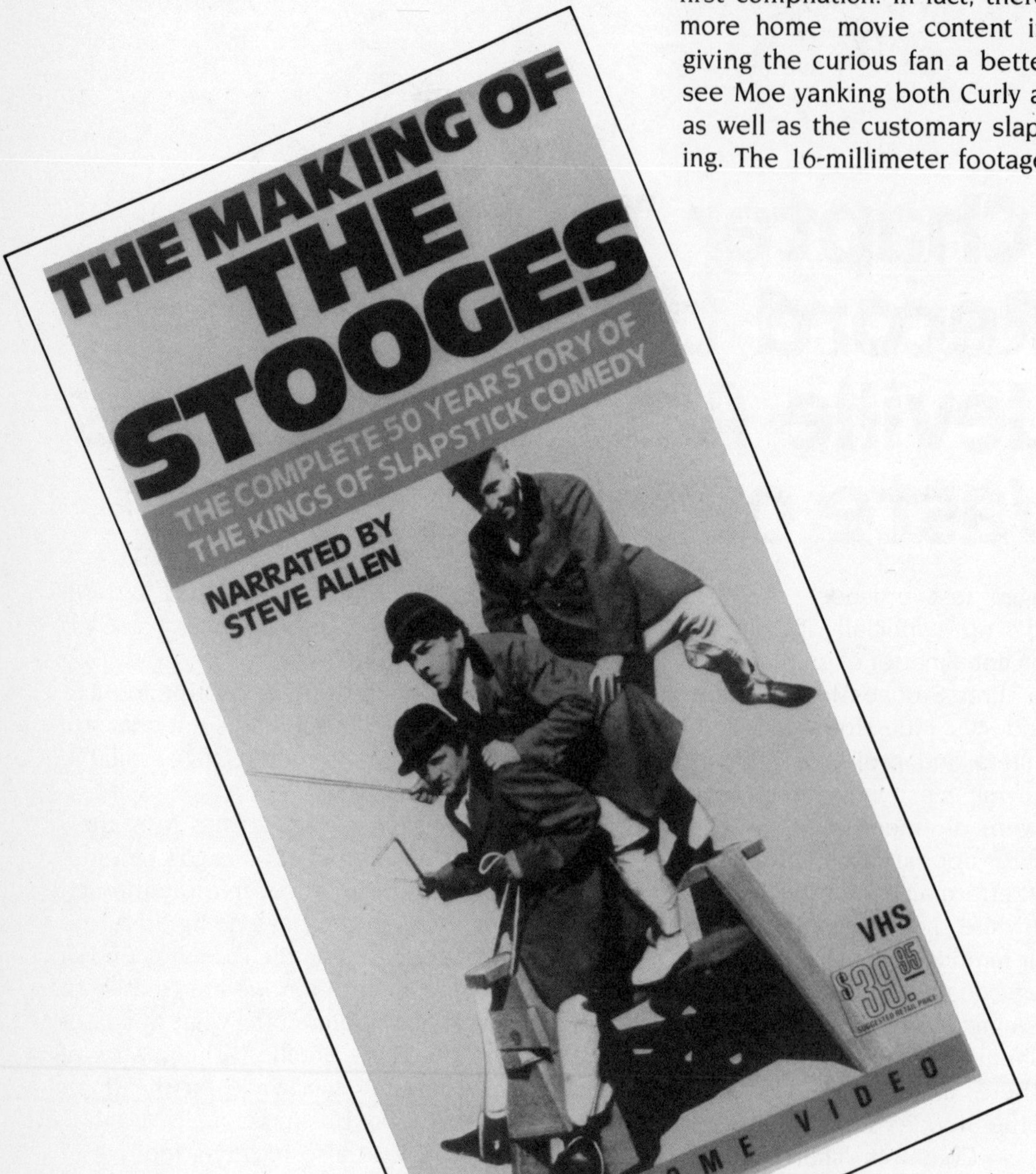

THE MAKING OF THE STOOGES

THE COMPLETE 50 YEAR STORY OF THE KINGS OF SLAPSTICK COMEDY

NARRATED BY STEVE ALLEN

VHS
$39.95
SUGGESTED RETAIL PRICE

KARL HOME VIDEO

Steve Allen is host of this film, which features "lost" footage from MGM as well as home movies of the team shot without sound. Obviously, when you're running around in circles on the floor you don't have to rely on words to express your feelings.

beginning of *Stoogephile* right after the film's opening credits.

If you're interested in getting a gander at this vaudeville footage, *The Making of the Stooges* is available from Lorimar Home Video at $39.95 through your local video store, or save $10 and get it from Channel 13 Video, P.O. Box 15602, North Hollywood, CA 91615. *The Stoogephile Trivia Movie* ($19.95) is an MPI Home Video release, and is also available at your local store. In addition, you can get *Stoogephile* by calling Fusion Video toll-free at 1-800-338-7710 and ordering with your VISA or MasterCard.

In addition to "lost" footage, this film features highlights from the Stooges' 1983 "Walk of Fame" ceremony in Hollywood. Joe Besser was on hand for the event, introduced by smart-aleck Milton Berle as "a man who was once a very big star."

Lost Anecdote #14
"Kidney-Stone Romeo"

When the Stooges were on the road in vaudeville, they were often separated from their families for long periods of time. So they had to plan special personal outings well in advance so as not to conflict with their live appearance schedule.

Babe Howard remembers the difficulty she and her husband had just trying to get some time off for their *honeymoon* in 1925, shortly after Shemp had joined up with Ted Healy. Shemp finally managed to get some free time, but wound up with an attack of kidney stones while on the trip.

Now, if you haven't been treated to a kidney-stone attack, it should be pointed out that the "stones'" gradual movement from kidney to urethra makes most bodily functions excruciatingly painful, and any kind of romancing downright impossible.

"But that was Shemp for you," said Babe with a laugh. "He always did have a hilarious sense of timing."

This snapshot is definitely *not* from Shemp and Babe's ill-fated honeymoon. The venerable Shemp is standing way too erect to be suffering from kidney stones.

Chapter Fourteen: "In Color We're Twice as Ugly as in Black and White"

The title of this chapter is an actual quote from Moe Howard, made in 1960 after the Stooges had begun toying with the idea of doing all of their subsequent film work in color.

As was pointed out in the previous chapter, getting your hands on *any* color footage of the Stooges is no mean feat. They only costarred in one color feature film (*Snow White and the Three Stooges*), and virtually all of their short subjects were shot in black and white.

But in 1960, the Stooges began work on their first color film project since their early, early Ted Healy films at MGM. This lost episode, titled *The Three Stooges Scrapbook*, is a never-released TV pilot that was originally produced with the intention of selling it to prime-time TV.

The long-term expectations for this film far outweighed the final outcome. Nevertheless, producer Norman Maurer (doubling as the Stooges' manager) planned to appease the P.T.A. by toning down the Stooges' roughhousing, as well as adding cartoon episodes to the live-action footage. These animated segments would feature the Stooges as cartoon charac-

ters, with Moe, Larry, and Joe DeRita providing their own voices.

The format was similar to that employed in their "New Three Stooges" comedy/cartoon series in 1965, but the performances, storyline, production values, and even photography were superior in *Scrapbook*. Moreover, as one can see, upon screening a rare print of this film in good condition, the color is noticeably sharper and will be distinctly enticing to Stooges fans accustomed to seeing the boys in black and white.

The full-color *Scrapbook* opens with a cartoon of the Stooges' talking heads, singing the show's theme song:

Larry, Moe, Curly Joe
They're the funniest guys I know
Golly Gee, that's for me
I wanna be a Stooge
Well you can be
Like those three
If you don't use common sense
Yes indeed
All you need
Is a high intelligence

Yes siree
They're the three
Musketeers of comedy
They have fun
We have fun
I wanna be a Stooge
Yeah!

Then, complete with obligatory canned laugh track and tiresome wacky music, we find the Stooges preparing dinner in the apartment. They're supposed to be bona fide TV stars, but

("roommates wanted") placed by an eccentric scientist, Dr. Do-lottle (Emil Sitka). The Doc lives in an enormous, castle-like place called Creepy Manor. It seems he has just invented a space carrier that looks like a cross between a helicopter, submarine, and tank. And when the boys arrive at Sitka's place, they find out just how Creepy the Manor is when the Doc reveals his suspicion that he's being hounded by a spy from outer space, whom he believes is trying to steal the plans for his contraption.

The boys reluctantly decide to help Sitka out,

The Stooges poised for the "Paginini" ("Page Nine") gag on the set of *The Three Stooges Scrapbook*.

they still live in a dump where no cooking is allowed. When the boys hear their landlady approaching, they scramble to hide the evidence. They use an elaborate, two-sided, flip-over coffee table and a false-fronted TV set to conceal their goodies.

But the landlady smells food, and when she opens the TV, out falls enough meat and produce to feed Rhode Island. She screams at the Stooges to hit the road, and they scurry out the door in search of a new place to live.

The boys eventually answer a newspaper ad

agreeing to spend the night at Creepy Manor. Larry and Joe share a bed in one room, while Moe sacks out in another right down the hall. But it's not long before the monster-like "alien spy" starts harassing Curly Joe from behind the bedroom wall while Larry snores away. Joe runs off to find Moe, leaving Larry to fend for himself with the green, hairy creature.

Then, the monster decides to take Larry's place in bed after carrying the sleeping Stooge off behind a sliding bookcase. "Oh, Mabel," Larry ad-libs, supposedly in his sleep, "You're

That's Emil Sitka in the monster getup. It seems the man who originally played the butler/monster part wasn't scary enough, so the Stooges called on old pal Sitka to do the dirty work.

here at last—you've swept me off my feet. . . ."

However, when Moe and Joe return, they subdue the monster, pull off its mask, and reveal—of course—Sitka's egg-bald butler.

The grateful Professor Do-lottle decides he can trust the Stooges enough to allow them to put his tank-helicopter-submarine into orbit. No, thanks, say the Stooges, you can keep your machine—we've got to get down to the TV station for our live broadcast!

The boys use just about every form of transportation to get to the studio—including parachute—and when they arrive just before airtime, they relate their story to the audience. They then open an oversized scrapbook loaded with Stooges photos, segueing into a cartoon adventure dealing with Columbus's discovery of America. When we return to the flesh-and-blood Stooges, they're arguing about whether the world is, or isn't, flat.

"Flat" is probably the best word to describe *Scrapbook*. Its entertainment value rests solely on its curiosity status. The film is hurriedly pro-duced, its content is rather childish in nature, and most of the gags of consequence are lifted from earlier, classic Stooges comedies (notably *Hot Scots* [1948]). Veteran scripter Elwood Ullman was on hand to write the teleplay, while his frequent partner, Ed Bernds, was conspicuously absent as director.

Norman Maurer did, however, hire a vastly experienced TV director, Sidney Miller, to run the show on *Scrapbook*. Miller himself recalls, "We shot it at Beechwood Studios and the street scenes outside the Charlie Chaplin Theatre on LaBrea Avenue. It couldn't have been shot in more than three days. And I remember

An outdoor shot like this might take up to a full hour to film, depending on the distractions such as honking car horns, airplanes, or a gust of wind under Moe's nightshirt.

the Stooges were very improvisational and well-seasoned."

Miller encouraged quite a bit of improvisation in the film; Emil Sitka remembers that, at the last moment, he was even asked to step into the role of the butler for the "alien spy" scenes:

"This guy that played the butler didn't know how to act menacing. In the costume, he looked like a kid at Halloween—funny, but not scary. So Norman said, 'Just leave it to Emil,' and I did the whole bit and they loved it."

In addition, says Sitka, "the guy that played the butler was an absolute double for Nikita Khrushchev. I discussed an idea with Elwood Ullman about a future episode in which the Stooges discover that it actually *is* Khrushchev spying on my plans. That would have been a good storyline, and Elwood saw that. And this wasn't like Larry with one of his wild ideas—Elwood really liked it!"

Sitka was always interested in making contributions toward the Stooges' projects, because his personal relationship with Moe Howard guaranteed him involvement in most of their films, TV or theatrical.

"In any pilot that I was in, there were certain promises made. With this one, the Professor role was to be a continuing character, if the series was sold. I seem to remember that there were some buyers for the pilot, too—but only in late-night time slots which weren't agreeable to Norman."

Spearheading the project, Norman Maurer screened it for various network executives and TV sponsors, but could not get a deal with which he felt comfortable. Ironically, this project was financed privately instead of by a particular sponsor or television company.

Despite Maurer's failure to unload the pilot, press releases and storyboards for the show dealt with the Stooges' fictional involvement in American history.

In one proposed episode, Larry loans George Washington a silver dollar. In another, Moe, "while mopping up the lab floor, yanks a clump of Larry's hair, leaving the curly filaments on the bench for Mr. Edison the next morning." And in yet another, Curly Joe keeps history on course as his "trusty cigar-lighter" torches the lamp in the tower for Paul Revere's signal.

Although the ideas were clever in concept, all of the network executives agreed they were unsuitable for prime-time programming.

"By this time, the Stooges were considered a kiddie property," says Jeff Lenburg, coauthor of the Citadel Press book, *The Three Stooges Scrapbook*, who worked closely with both Maurer and his wife Joan Howard. "That was the biggest problem. It didn't sell because it was kiddie-oriented for prime time and the show wouldn't have a broad enough market."

Although the pilot was never sold to TV, a portion of the cost was recouped when much of the footage was written into the screenplay of the Stooges' 1962 Columbia feature, *The Three Stooges in Orbit*. The unsold *Scrapbook* footage was reprocessed from color to black and white and simply incorporated into the feature film storyline. Ed Bernds was the director who helmed the entire project.

However, in 1963, Columbia Pictures issued a shortened version of *Scrapbook*—in color—to theaters across the country as a featurette, or filler, like the two-reelers of years past.

Today, though, fans are forced to rely on faded, reddening prints of *Scrapbook* if they want to see it at all. These ten-minute versions occasionally float from collector to collector, so we'd suggest contacting the Three Stooges Fan Club at 710 Collins Avenue, Lansdale, Pennsylvania 19446, for details.

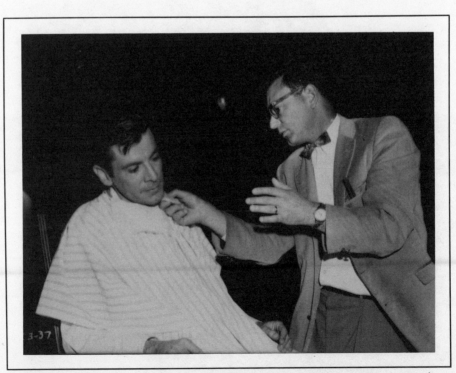

Producer Norman Maurer is made up for a cameo appearance in *Scrapbook*.

Norman Maurer (right) "holds up" production trying to secure the fish bowl for the table-turning gag.

"Wait a minute, now, I've almost got it. . . ."

"Spread out, you numbskulls! I'll handle this!"

C3-75

"Success!"

C3-71

And all that trouble for a three-second gag!

Lost Anecdote #15
"Flips, Grunts, and Groans"

The year after the Stooges completed *The Three Stooges Scrapbook*, they began work on their most financially successful feature ever, *The Three Stooges Meet Hercules* (1962). During shooting, director Ed Bernds remembers an accident that occurred that almost spelled the end of the Three Stooges!

Apparently, Moe ran up a flight of stairs so fast he stumbled and was literally propelled into a backward flip! Norman Maurer later told Bernds, "I thought to myself, 'There goes my father-in-law.' "

But the entire crew groaned in relief as Moe emerged just slightly shaken from the whole thing. That's no small accomplishment considering he was almost 65 years old at the time.

Apparently, once a Stooge, always a Stooge—it's just too bad they didn't catch Moe's accidental acrobatics on film!

Chapter Fifteen: "The Attractions Are Coming, The Attractions Are Coming . . ."

When the Stooges began starring in their own tailor-made features, Columbia Pictures began assembling "coming attractions" films—or "trailers"—to promote their forthcoming movies. And since these little films have not been seen in theaters in years—or *ever* on TV, for that matter—they are now regarded as "lost episodes."

The good news is that you can still see a handful of these trailers completely intact, in a number of recently released home videocassettes.

The boys' first starring film trailer with Joe DeRita, promoting *Have Rocket, Will Travel* (1959), can be seen in *The Making of the Stooges*. The trailer features highlights from the film, as well as wacky voice-over narration like "You've heard of the Sputnik and Nutnik—now here's the laugh-nick," and "It's a Three-Stooge riot on a three-stage rocket." Remember, we said it's *wacky*, not *funny*.

On the more inventive side is the trailer for *The Outlaws Is Coming* (1965), the Stooges' last feature film. In fact, the title *The Outlaws Is Coming* is itself a parody of the actual promo-

tional campaign for Alfred Hitchcock's *The Birds* (" 'The Birds' Is Coming."). In the trailer for this one, we are treated to stop-motion photography, special effects, and other gimmicks not seen in the feature itself. This trailer turns up in *The Stoogephile Trivia Movie*.

Even though the trailers for *Have Rocket* and *Outlaws* heavily emphasize the Stooges, they are practically ignored in the promotional film for *Snow White and the Three Stooges*, their 1961 Technicolor feature for 20th Century–Fox. This is strange, because it was quite obviously the Stooges whom Fox was relying on to bring in the kids. Nevertheless, the trailer is in full color, and it gives a pretty good indication of the actual content of *Snow White*—very little Stooges slapstick but plenty of storybook trimmings. This one is included in *The Joy of Stooge-ing*.

The Stooges don't have much to do in *Four for Texas* (1963), either, but they are featured prominently in that film's trailer. The boys were hired as "guest stars" for this Frank Sinatra-Dean Martin romp, performing their age-old "Point to the Right" routine in front of a crowd of spectators, with Martin serving as the straight man. In

The boys as real-life "coming attractions"—on KPLR-TV/Channel 11 in St. Louis in the early 1960s—to promote a local personal appearance. "Captain Eleven" is actually ex-vaudevillian Harry Fender, an old pal of the Stooges.

fact, a portion of that routine is included in the trailer, highlighted by a freeze-frame on Moe, Larry, and Curly Joe getting the triple-slap from Dino. This trailer also turns up in *The Stoogephile Trivia Movie* as well as *The Joy of Stooge-ing.*

In addition to these "Curly Joe" trailers, the promotional film for a Curly Howard compilation, *Stop, Look and Laugh* (1960), is also now available on home video. The trailer features clips from Columbia short subjects *Oily to Bed, Oily to Rise* (1939), *How High Is Up?* (1940), *Sock-A-Bye Baby* (1942), *What's the Matador?* (1942), *Micro-Phonies* (1945), and *Half-Wits Holiday* (1947), as well as footage of host Paul Winchell, his dummies, and the Marquis Chimps. This one is also available in *The Making of the Stooges.*

In addition to these commercial promotional films, the Stooges also made a promotional short for the U.S. Government in 1968. Titled *Star Spangled Salesman,* the film, produced and directed by Norman Maurer, was a coventure between Columbia and 20th Century–Fox made specifically for the U.S. Treasury Department. The idea behind this project was to convince employers and employees alike to join the Treasury's Payroll Savings Plan.

Moe, Larry, and Joe DeRita are featured along with Carl Reiner (host), Milton Berle, Carol Burnett, and other television personalities in this entertaining short. Maurer manages to sugarcoat the hard sell with plenty of comedy, as comedian Howard Morris wanders around a busy film studio signing up employees for the "Plan."

The Stooges are lighting technicians on a lunch break, ready to devour an enormous submarine sandwich when Morris makes his entrance. Although he attempts to convince the Stooges of the merits of Payroll Savings, the boys wind up convincing themselves, and are falling all over each other to sign up. The Stooges' scene is brief and Morris is on to other employees just moments after meeting the Stooges.

Footage of the Stooges' scene from *Star Spangled Salesman* appears in *The Stoogephile Trivia Movie,* during a segment titled "The Curly Joe Fitness Plan" (Joe's gut is enormous in this one). You can get a copy of *The Stoogephile* at your local video store, or by calling Fusion Video toll-free at 1-800-338-7710 and ordering with your VISA or MasterCard. You can order *The Joy of Stooge-ing* from Fusion as well, which contains the episode in its entirety.

Joe DeRita on the verge of performing "The Curly Joe Shuffle." From *Star Spangled Salesman.*

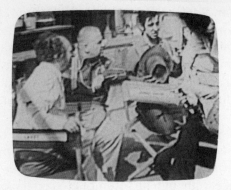

The boys caucus on the set of *The Outlaws Is Coming*. According to Emil Sitka, the Stooges hated being called "the boys." "Dupes," "boobs," "saps," "idiots," "half-wits" . . . *anything* was acceptable but *boys*.

Curly Joe and Larry have just tasted Moe's cactus cooler on the set of *The Outlaws Is Coming*.

You'll notice Moe isn't gagging, but then, you'll notice Moe isn't *drinking*, either.

"How does a nice bowl cut grab you?"

Moe attempts to re-part producer Norman Maurer's hair on the set of *The Outlaws Is Coming*.

Lay off the dairy, Joe, or the next thing you know you'll be in need of the Curly Joe Fitness Plan. As seen in *The Stoogephile Trivia Movie*.

Lost Anecdote #16
"Yes, We All Have Pajamas"

By the time the Stooges were starring in features in the late 1950s, their fans wanted to know everything about them, so they prepared an official press release in 1960.

One personal question often asked of major celebrities is "Do you sleep in the nude?" Well, thankfully, Moe Howard would have none of that. According to that official biography interview, the Head Stooge stated that he slept in "full uniform," meaning uppers and lowers of pajamas, but never slept under the covers even in the coldest of weather.

In addition, the Ornery One claimed he never wore a topcoat "no matter what the weather."

Any further questions?

Chapter Sixteen: "Hi, This Is Milton Berle's Brother—Have You Gotta Minute?"

When the Stooges' theatrical films were first released to TV in 1958, the boys became overnight television stars. The video premiere of their old Columbia shorts made feature-length excursions like *Have Rocket, Will Travel* a profitable reality, rather than just another Moe Howard "I-wish-we-were-Abbott-and-Costello" pipe dream.

Despite the fact that the old two-reelers turned up on TV in the late '50s, ABC Television had actually made an arrangement with Columbia Pictures as early as 1949 for the rights to seventy-eight Three Stooges shorts starring Curly Howard. ABC never exercised that right, so Columbia decided to sell their Stooge package via syndication nine years later.

However, when the Stooges originally got wind of ABC's plans to air their old films, they decided to produce their own brand-new project for that network—a pilot film that would be shot before a live audience. The boys hoped to use the pilot as a means of obtaining a weekly slot for their slapstick antics.

The series was to be titled "The Three Stooges," and would star Moe, Larry, and Shemp along with Emil Sitka and Columbia stalwart Symona Boniface as regulars. A deal was struck and a complete half-hour-for-broadcast film was produced at ABC Studios in Hollywood, shot before a wildly appreciative live audience. Milton Berle's brother, Phil Berle, served as producer (Norman Maurer was still drawing comic books), and Moe's old pal, comedy writer Henry Taylor, assembled the gag-laden script.

The film, titled *Jerks of All Trades*, is, unfortunately, about as unfunny as the Three Stooges get. There's almost no pacing throughout and the Stooges' timing is in itself sloppy. But the Stooge-happy audience really seems to get off on it nevertheless.

As for the cast, Emil Sitka and Symona Boniface are quite good (both were seasoned stage pros) and, strangely enough, it's Larry who really stands out among the Stooges. He's the most relaxed of the trio, most of his comedy reads,

Emil Sitka, from the set of *The Three Stooges in Orbit* (1962), still playing the befuddled fall guy. Sitka was promised a regular role on the Stooges' 1940s TV project if it sold to a network to air on a weekly basis.

and he's a pleasant, lively contrast to the mechanical approach of both Moe and Shemp. In this live stuff, Shemp is bland and dumb in a tired, robot-like manner. Moe is stiff, overbearing, and screechy, much more so than usual. But Larry acts as if he's running through a rehearsal in somebody's living room, which is probably why, when he behaved this way in the team's movie appearances, he simply looked as if he didn't know what in hell he was doing. Larry is funnier than ever in the live stuff, playing it with such an off-the-cuff goofiness that he really *is* much funnier than he is in his film appearances. It looks as though Larry's refusal to rehearse or even devote minimal attention to his craft paid off in this case; his performance is as spontaneous as a Stooges fan could hope for.

In fact, probably the funniest bit of business in the film occurs when Larry tries to roll up a window shade during a scene in which the boys attempt to ''redecorate'' Sitka's house. The mechanics of the gag obviously aren't working as we find Larry contending with a roll-up shade that just won't roll up. Unable to improvise his way out of it, he continues playing with the shade over and over, trying to get it to cooperate. The audience, of course, doesn't have a clue as to what's going on. Meanwhile, the camera remains static on Larry struggling mightily with the shade, obscuring Moe's and Shemp's antics upstage! Finally, with an attitude of ''let's get this thing over with,'' Moe grabs a conveniently placed custard pie and whips it at Shemp.

In addition to this tomfoolery, the show is loaded with way too many jokes (almost none of which pay off) and stupid slapstick that is more childish and irritating than funny. If people who hate the Stooges are exposed only to stuff like this, it's no wonder they can't stand them. Almost all of the physical interaction is slipshod and poorly timed, including a celery fight that is so babyish and contrived one actually feels sorry for the Stooges. (Why are these old pros *doing* this crap?) Special pity is reserved for Shemp Howard, one of the funniest men who ever lived, for his participation in this embarrassing effort—even though he seems to be only half-awake during the proceedings. For the first time on record, the legendary Three Stooges—by this time well-seasoned veterans of the stage, screen, and just about everything else—actually look amateurish. It's no surprise this was one pilot that never got off the ground.

Originally, and perhaps with some foresight, Shemp wanted no part of the TV project, and attempted to bow out. The story goes that Larry called his pal Mousie Garner and asked him to replace Shemp for the TV appearances. Mousie was doing a lot of TV in those days (he eventually became a frequent guest on ''The Colgate Comedy Hour''), and was quite interested in joining the Three Stooges. But while he was mulling over the possibility of doing *Jerks of All Trades*, Shemp agreed to go ahead with the deal after all, and The Mouse was out of the picture.

For interested parties, the Three Stooges pilot, *Jerks of All Trades*, is available in its entirety in *The Stooges: Lost and Found* ($19.95), a compilation film consisting of lost Stooges episodes intended for, or originally aired on, TV. The film is a Madhouse Video release and can be ordered on VHS or Beta from Fusion Video at 1-800-338-7710. Use your VISA or MasterCard when ordering via the toll-free number.

Several years after the failure of *Jerks*, the Stooges took another crack at TV, this time with more successful results. On March 11, 1950, Moe, Larry, and Shemp appeared live on CBS's "Camel Comedy Caravan," "The Ed Wynn Show," sponsored by Camel Cigarettes. The boys play meddling network executives, Mr. C., B., and S.: Larry in charge of soap operas, spewing bubbles from his mouth; Shemp in charge of cutting costs as well as Wynn's necktie; and Moe in charge of Larry and Shemp. As per usual, the Stooges interrupt sketches, fight with each other, and destroy scenery, as the flakey Wynn struggles desperately to get rid of them.

The Stooges' scenes are jam-packed with chestnuts, including a backfiring fountain pen, the cramming-three-in-a-phone-booth gag, and the "double zinger," where, at Moe's command, Larry and Shemp ram their eyes into Wynn's extended fingers. This lost episode, which co-stars actor William Frawley and singer Helen Forrest, is again on the bizarre side—even though the Stooges are given the opportunity to do their stuff, it's shot in front of a studio audience and, therefore, devoid of sound effects. Unfortunately, the absence of the exaggerated effects only draws attention to the sheer lameness of much of their clowning. By eliminating the farcical frosting, it looks a lot like three old guys hurting each other without any cartoonish payoff.

By the late 1960s, the Stooges were already 20-year veterans of television. Here, Martha Raye seems to be "doing" Joe Besser in a Stooges television appearance from 1965.

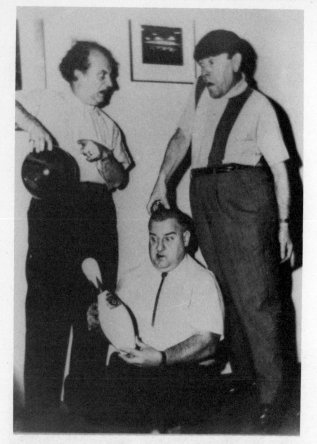

This black-and-white snapshot seems to refute Moe's claim that the Stooges were twice as ugly in color. It's just too difficult to imagine them being any uglier than they are right here.

The highlight of the film, however, is the finale, where Wynn convinces the Stooges to sing. They break into a three-part harmony rendition of "When You Wore a Tulip," while Wynn wanders around the stage, cueing stagehands to drop sandbags on their heads. The stagehands keep missing the Stooges, still vocalizing, but they wind up beaning Wynn with one enormous bag. Ed is knocked more senseless than usual, and the curtain closes on both Wynn and his "unwanted" guests.

The sandbag gag had its roots in the Stooges' days with Ted Healy. He used an almost identical routine in his vaudeville appearances with them; twenty-five years later it was still getting respectable laughs.

The Stooges' appearance on "The Ed Wynn Show" is also available in *The Stooges: Lost and Found* from Madhouse Video. Order it from

Fusion Video by calling toll-free 1-800-338-7710 and using your VISA or MasterCard.

The Stooges became more and more comfortable on TV with each subsequent appearance. And by the time they did CBS's "The Frank Sinatra Show" (1952), they really had their TV legs. The boys were guest stars on Sinatra's gala New Year's Eve special, also starring Yvonne DeCarlo and Louis Armstrong. The Stooges even managed to work longtime foil Vernon Dent into the action, in which they play temporary servants at Sinatra's swingin' party.

The boys virtually steal the show with their nonstop buffoonery. Moe dances with Sinatra. Larry dances with a female guest, but on the sofa. Shemp doesn't do any dancing, but has a seizure, falls to the floor, and runs around in a circle on his shoulder. The Stooges fall over furniture. They throw the guests' coats out the window. They even mix a cocktail in Vernon Dent's mouth. (What's Vernon Dent doing at a party of Frank Sinatra's?)

They try out some new stuff. Like a triple Lionel Barrymore impersonation performed in unison. Like a one-time Shemp routine in which

Judging by Moe's expression, you *know* something violent is going to happen. Ed Wynn follows Moe's tips, both of which will ultimately wind up in Shemp's eyes. From "The Ed Wynn Show."

MOE: "Come on, Frankie—when do we get to dance?"
SINATRA: "You'll have to wait 'til the girls get here."

MOE: "Well, then I won't get to dance with *you*!" Larry's reaction seems appropriate in this scene from the "Frank Sinatra Show."

he tries to take off a jacket without spilling two handfuls of drinks. They even toss in an inside joke in which they tell Sinatra they'll be at "Charlie Foy's"—a supper club owned by one of the Seven Little Foys who was also a pal of the Stooges'.

The Stooges' stuff is enhanced by the fact that Sinatra makes a pretty affable "straight" to their nonsense, even laying them out with a nice, crisp triple slap halfway through the show.

Despite the Stooges' antics, the show is a typical early-TV mess. It's plagued with missed entrances and exits, misfired sound effects, and camerawork completely avoiding the action, focusing instead on Sinatra's reactions to what's going on out of frame. But in a way, that's part of what makes watching this show so enjoyable. In an age of ultra-slick, pre-recorded television, it's fun to watch the live TV of yesterday, with all its inadequacies and mistakes. And it's a riot seeing the Stooges ad-lib their way out of one catastrophe after another. You'll love the scene where all three turn toward the door in reaction to a doorbell, long before the sound effects man remembers to ring it.

This lost episode is definitely a must for any fan of the Stooges or live television.

The Stooges' appearance on "The Frank Sinatra Show" is available on home video in a compilation tape called "TV Jitters." You can get your hands on the tape by sending $24.95 in check or money order, or by sending your VISA/ MasterCard number, to: Channel 13 Video, P.O. Box 15602, N. Hollywood, CA 91615.

Lost Anecdote #17
"Saved from the Belle"

During the 1950s, when the boys weren't doing TV or making shorts at Columbia, they were on the road making personal appearances. Vaudeville was all but dead, but the Stooges could still command a decent buck making appearances at various movie theaters around the country.

Mickey Gold, former usher at the old Oriental Theatre in Chicago, remembers seeing Moe slapping Larry and Shemp around with such gusto, "you could see the spit flying out of their mouths." When he went backstage and asked Shemp how he could stand getting cracked around like that, Shemp replied, "I'm made of cement."

But apparently Shemp's heart wasn't made of cement, as he phoned his wife daily from the road just to check up on the family.

In fact, his wife Babe remembered that she actually gave him the go-ahead for extra-marital activity when he was touring. "I told him, if it happens, it happens. Don't worry about it, you're only human. But I found out later that Shemp would have no part of fooling around because, for one thing, he was scared to death of disease. Curly was in and out of one VD clinic after another, and I know that Shemp didn't want to have anything to do with something that might make him sick. He hated being sick; he was frightened to death of it."

But once Shemp's old pal/tormenter Ted Healy got wind of Shemp's attitude, he was obsessed with embarrassing him just for laughs. According to Babe Howard, Ted frequently hired prostitutes to practically attack Shemp backstage, tearing at his clothes and coming on to him like there was no tomorrow. Babe even broke up one such would-be "tryst," giving Healy a piece of her mind in the aftermath. Shemp himself thought the "jokes" were more tacky than funny, but Ted thought they were a ball as long as they got a rise out of Shemp.

Chapter Seventeen:
"Okay, but Only if You Promise Not to Hit Me"

In 1955, just as the Stooges' TV career was gaining momentum, Shemp Howard died suddenly in late November. He was in a taxicab with a couple of pals and in the middle of telling a joke, when he suddenly slumped forward into a friend's lap, burning the man with his cigar. Shemp was dead of a massive heart attack at age 60.

"That's the strange thing," said Babe Howard more than twenty-five years later. "Here Shemp was scared to death of being sick, and dying, and when he did go it was quick and painless and he was laughing and having fun with his friends. He never knew what was happening. Can you think of a better way to go than that?"

The grieving Moe Howard considered folding the Three Stooges once and for all. But Larry, who freely blew his Stooges paychecks and was subsequently broke, persuaded Moe to continue the act with a new third man. Columbia Pictures lined the Stooges up with one of their contract players, burlesque and vaudeville veteran Joe Besser, and the boys were back in business by early 1956.

But Joe made a couple of provisions before joining the team. He insisted that his contract include a clause preventing Moe or Larry from slapping, hitting, or in any way hurting him. Joe did not like receiving-end slapstick, and he made damn sure nobody was going to smack him around against his will.

Moe and Larry had no objection whatsoever to that request. In fact, Larry even told Joe that he was used to getting beaten up for a living, and would gladly take twice as much punishment to make up for Besser.

So the new Three Stooges—Moe, Larry, and Joe—embarked on a series of sixteen two-reelers made over a period of two years (1956–58). All of their films together are in release to TV through the Columbia Stooges shorts package.

However, like Shemp Howard before him, Joe Besser made a number of solo starring shorts for Columbia throughout the late 1940s and early '50s. One of his earliest, *Fraidy Cat* (1951), directed by Jules White, is actually a remake of White's Three Stooges two-reeler *Dizzy Detectives* (1943). The other Besser solo efforts are also Stoogey in nature; and since all but one were

Dapper Joe Besser about ten years prior to joining the Stooges. Little did he know. . . .

directed by White, they are also rather violent and occasionally very crude. White loved to employ cruel slapstick whenever possible, and he often relied on it as a means of injecting action or excitement into a scene that was otherwise emotionally "flat."

A typical example is *Caught on the Bounce* (1953), which is about as lame as any of the Jules White Stooge shorts of that same period. The film features the usual quota of Jules's cruelty-to-women gags, with the truly nice Maxine Gates character on the receiving end of some pretty mean "fat" jokes. Jules loved to portray hefty women in humiliating situations, which in this case are almost all in poor taste. And to top it off, the climax of the story takes place on the exact same set used in that Stooge Short from Hell, *Cuckoo on a Choo Choo* (1952), perhaps the team's least entertaining short subject.

Bounce gives Joe Besser a comedy family, with Maxine as Mama and Edward Coch, Jr. as Junior.

Coch looks like a nine-year-old Jackie Gleason, thus completing Jules's concept of Joe heading a completely overweight family. Jules, a slightly-built man who loved to show off his ribs by directing films with his shirt off, apparently had little tolerance for obesity and loved to make fun of it wherever possible. And good taste never stood in the venerable producer's way if he was in search of an outrageous gag. In this one, Maxine gets her buttocks caught in a chair when her weight crushes the seat. Later, on the train, she falls from her upper berth and literally flattens a helpless porter in the hall. And finally, she's supposedly so fat her berth eventually caves in, landing on top of husband Joe and Junior in the lower. "Did somebody drop an atom bomb?" asks Junior. "Yeah," replies Joe, "a blonde one!"

Aside from fat jokes, there is the usual Jules White quantity of extremely protracted gags. For example, Junior cuts a wad of chewing tobacco into rectangular chunks and sticks them inside a box of fudge. Joe, of course, proceeds to eat them, giving Jules an opportunity to work in one of his favorite gags, the face-turns-white, I-think-I'm-gonna-puke bit. In some of these episodes, it looks as if Jules simply dreamt the action and then attempted to translate it as a story; the films have an unintentionally contrived aura that is almost funny in itself. But if you don't get a kick out of "bad" farce, then none of the Jules White "Joe Besser Series" films will provide much entertainment.

Besser did, however, make one starring short under Ed Bernds's direction—*Waiting in the Lurch*, released in 1949 and scripted by Elwood Ullman. The script, which dealt with Joe's obsession with chasing fire engines, was a favorite of Ullman's. It was the veteran screenwriter's only film with Besser, and he mentioned it frequently in interviews. The content of that film is, however, inaccessible; as of this writing a print has not been obtained for review.

None of the Joe Besser solo films are currently in release on TV or home video, but serious Besser-obsessers might try contacting the Three Stooges Fan Club at 710 Collins Avenue, Lansdale, Pennsylvania 19446, for help in locating prints.

No, this isn't the "Night Gallery." These are actually blow-ups from the existing ultra-grainy kinescope of *Jerks of All Trades*, the quintessential "lost episode." From the looks of *these* mugs, perhaps somebody "lost" the film on purpose.

Joe Besser was a smash hit at the unveiling of the Stooges' star on the "Walk of Fame" in 1983.

Lost Anecdote #18
"No Joe, Boys"

The induction of Joe Besser into the Stooges only made keeping their names straight that much more difficult. As most Stooge fans are well aware, Curly Howard had replaced Shemp Howard in 1932. Then Shemp replaced Curly in 1946. Joe Besser then replaced Shemp ten years later, and then Joe DeRita stepped in for Joe Besser *two* years later. Sound confusing? Of course it does, even if you're a compulsive Stoogemaniac. The Stooges themselves saw the constant changes in personnel as potentially confusing, especially to their younger fans. So they decided to clarify the situation by giving Joe DeRita a nickname.

Joe himself explained the premise behind rechristening him "Curly Joe," during an interview in 1987: "I was named Curly Joe so it wouldn't confuse the kiddies. We didn't want them to mix me up with Curly Howard or with Joe Besser. Calling me Curly Joe separated me from both of them."

So he wasn't Curly. And he wasn't Joe Besser, either. Maybe they should have called him Curly Joe DeShemp, and got all *three* names in there.

Chapter Eighteen: "See, I Always *Told* You I Was the Funny One!"

It would seem that Stooges like Joe Besser and Shemp enjoyed the most prolific solo careers—at least in terms of material on record. But the busiest solo Stooge of all may have been Moe Howard. Long before he had thoughts of becoming a comedian, Moe was actually a child actor, appearing in silent films shot on Long Island, as well as in a series of twelve two-reel sports comedies filmed in Pittsburgh, starring Honus Wagner. "These pictures I never saw," said Moe in an interview many years later. "I think perhaps they made banjo picks out of the film, I don't know."

Well, *all* of Moe's solo work as a single didn't end up that way—his first solo film as an adult was recently unearthed by members of the Three Stooges Fan Club! It's titled *Give a Man a Job* (1933), and was shot at MGM as a Depression-era public service film for the NRA (National Recovery Administration).

This musical comedy short, like many produced during the Depression, was made to remind people to hire the unemployed.

It opens with star Jimmy Durante singing the title song, and then quizzing his audience about what they've done for the cause. During the course of this sequence we find Moe, with slicked-back hair, as a pest exterminator watching Durante's presentation.

Durante tells him, "You must give your assistants each a nice weekend's vacation!"

Moe half-heartedly exclaims, "Then I'll need more men to kill the rats!"

"But we *want* you to hire a crowd!" Durante yells. "You'll do good work if you hang out this sign [reading NRA]. It means no rats allowed!"

Fans can contact the Three Stooges Fan Club, 710 Collins Avenue, Lansdale, Pennsylvania 19446, for more information on how to get a look at this early curiosity piece.

You might think it peculiar seeing Moe in an essentially "straight" role and with his hair combed like a businessman—but wait until you've seen him in *Strictly for Laffs* (1961). This is perhaps his most peculiar solo appearance, a guest shot on a pilot for a TV series to be hosted by comedian Dave Barry.

Shot on film, this never-aired demo features Moe and two other guest comedians performing for a small live audience. The program

At age 70, Moe tried to change his image as the Mean Stooge.

Would you buy a used boat from this man?

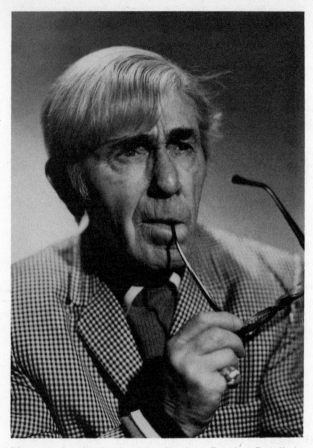

Moe as he looked while filming *Doctor Death* in 1973.

consists of host Barry and his guests sitting around a table chatting, trading one-liners, drinking coffee, and chain-smoking. Meanwhile, five women surround the "boys" on couches, smiling and giggling at appropriate moments.

As for Moe's contribution, he tells a story about a hunting trip in Canada, only to have Barry clumsily step on almost all of his punch-lines. The solo Stooge tries to cover for Barry's ineptitude by continuing with his routine, but the host manages to louse up Moe's timing so effectively that the whole monologue loses momentum and eventually just falls apart.

In addition, Moe appears a bit ill at ease working solo and out of the confines of his character—he's basically playing himself, not the "Moe" of the Three Stooges. He admits that it's very tough being a standup comedian because he's so accustomed to having a guy on each side of him to knock around. "Then again," he confesses, "I was thirty-five before I knew a pie was made to eat!"

Moe's appearance in *Strictly for Laffs* is available complete in *The Joy of Stooge-ing*, as well as in edited form in *The Stoogephile Trivia Movie*. Both are $19.95 each and are available from Fusion Video. You can order with your VISA or Master-Card by calling Fusion toll-free at 1-800-338-7710.

But Moe Howard's last screen appearance was in a low-budget horror movie titled *Doctor Death, Seeker of Souls* (1973), which is now available from Prism Home Video. Emil Sitka recalls seeing the film at a drive-in theater and thinking, "My God, is that *Moe*?" adding that Moe's appearance was "rather pathetic." In this one Moe plays a bit part as a horny old character who gets a thrill out of touching the elbow of a dead woman.

Doctor Death is available from Channel 13 Video through a special arrangement with Prism. You can obtain it by sending $49.95 in check or money order to: Channel 13 Video, P.O. Box 15602, N. Hollywood, CA 91615.

Lost Anecdote #19
"A Bard in the Head"

Moe Howard loved performing solo almost as much as he loved Shakespeare—in fact, he started his career playing virtually every one of old Will's most famous characters. The Shakespearean Stooge once played the title role in "Hamlet," although Moe himself stated that when he did it, "it was more like omelet."

Even when working with the Stooges, Moe was still obsessed with Shakespeare. During the Stooges' personal appearances, Moe would often begin reciting, "Friends! Romans! And countrymen! Lend me your ears," at which point he'd grab the other two jerks by their lobes and pull on them until they retaliated by bopping Moe on the head.

To date, however, there have been no reports of ground shaking or rumbling at the Bard's grave at Stratford-on-Avon.

Moe's cheery smile always brightened a movie set. When doing comedy, he was, like most great comedians, all business. He took Stoogeing as seriously as Shakespeare.

Chapter Nineteen: "Look, Fella, I'm Minsky's Top Banana—Don't Tell *Me* How to Be Funny!"

Moe Howard knows this guy will make a great Stooge, and so does Larry Fine. One look at his solo films and they know they're on the right track.

He's got Curly's build, Shemp's hair, and Joe Besser's disposition. And he has so much physical energy Stooge fans will barely recognize him as Joe DeRita. But here he is, in the flesh, all two-hundred-plus pounds of it, in a rollicking series of shorts made for Columbia in the late 1940s, a good ten or more years before becoming an official Stooge.

The films are mostly reworked efforts of other comedians. DeRita, at that time a top banana in burlesque (and you'll see why after checking out these shorts), was brought in to do a handful of curtain-raisers for Columbia's comedy department. And DeRita had definite ideas about the boss:

"Jules White was a schmuck. He wanted me to act like Curly. I told him I do my own thing, my own type of comedy. I don't imitate *nobody!*"

True, Joe's character resembles not so much Curly as Shemp or Joe Besser, if one must make a comparison. Of the handful of Columbia shorts DeRita made in the 40s—*Slappily Married* (1946), *The Good Bad Egg* (1947), *Wedlock Deadlock* (1947), and *Jitter Bughouse* (1948)—*Married* stands out in particular as a legitimately hilarious entry into Columbia's shorts series, and a true indication of DeRita's deserved status as the consummate burly-cue comic.

The film, directed by Ed Bernds and with a story by Elwood Ullman and Monty Collins, has Joe playing a man scared to death of Friday the Thirteenth. Sure enough, everything goes wrong, and there's some genuinely funny, wild slapstick in Joe's kitchen as he tries to cook breakfast for himself and wife Christine McIntyre (which is a laugh in itself).

But things go from bad to worse. At his dress shop—yes, in this one Curly Joe owns a women's clothing store—he runs afoul of a jealous palooka (played by Dick Wessel) and his pushy

By the 1940s, Joe DeRita was Harold Minsky's top banana, making him the "biggest" comic in burlesque.

primary exposure to his talents—ten years earlier, Joe could have made the perfect Stooge.

But making the DeRita Columbia shorts wasn't as much fun as it looked. Director Bernds remembers Joe as "a pain in the ass, always whining," a trait that apparently didn't change much by the time he was working with the Stooges in the late 1950s. So giving credit where credit's due, our hats are off to that master of pulling tricks out of the bag, Edward Bernds, for turning out some excellent work with a guy whose only previous movie exposure was a small role in an obscure feature titled *The Dough Girls* (1944).

On the opposite end of the pole is the rather hokey and predictable *The Good Bad Egg*, directed by Jules White from a Felix Adler script. The whole short is basically a long anecdote told by Joe to farmer Vernon Dent about why he despises eggs. It seems that Emil Sitka has talked his lonely bachelor pal, inventor Joe, into answering a marriage proposal written on an egg! Soon enough, Joe finds himself caught up in a marriage-for-profit racket where his new wife and monster-stepson Rudolph are not only in complete control of his wallet, but are apparently bent on ruining his life as well.

Joe finds nothing but headaches after his new wife and son move in with him. Like the Joe Besser solo films, this short runs the gamut of mean Jules White gags with little genuinely funny material. The climax comes when Rudolph secretly replaces the rotary spinner in Joe's new knee-action washing machine with a push-lawnmower blade. When Joe demonstrates his new invention for the stockholders of an investment company, everything goes up for grabs as the guests, including Symona Boniface, are plastered with wet laundry as it comes spewing out of the machine. Joe retaliates by stuffing Rudolph into the washer, slamming the lid shut and sitting on top of it as he "washes" Rudolph, cackling wildly.

This and the other three Joe DeRita solo shorts are still under Columbia's copyright, but, unfortunately, none of them have been released to TV or home video. Serious DeRita fans might try contacting the Three Stooges Fan Club for some information on how to obtain prints of these films.

girlfriend (Dorothy Granger). An accident results in Dorothy's passing out right into Joe's arms. Christine shows up, sees Joe with "another woman," and promptly leaves him to take up residence at the Hotel Amazon. This joint is run by the bitchy Symona Boniface and the butchy Helen Dickson, whom Stooges fans will recognize from some of their favorite "Curly" episodes. These two make life tough for Joe, who has to don drag in order to get past the tough female security guard (Dickson) and upstairs to explain things to his wife. From there on out the action gets wilder and the laughs build in typically Berndsian fashion.

If your only exposure to Joe DeRita is as a member of the Stooges, you're in for a treat with *Slappily Married*. His energy level is much higher (remember he's also much younger), and, if you really dig wild slapstick farce, he's about as funny as it gets. It's easy to see why Moe and Larry wanted him to join up if this was their

Posing for publicity stills can be a "drag," but the boys were more than happy to don women's clothing for the sake of their art. Joe DeRita made a particularly unconvincing "dame" in *Slappily Married* (1946).

Lost Anecdote #20
"An Ache in Every Cake"

Working with Joe DeRita could be full of surprises—as Emil Sitka discovered while shooting an episode of "The New Three Stooges" TV series in 1965.

"We were filming at an outdoor restaurant and I was playing a customer who was unhappy with the Stooges' service," says Sitka. "So I'm in a thing where I'm supposed to slap Joe a number of times, and each time make the slap a little harder. Well, there are ways of doing this kind of thing where you just kind of fake it and you don't really have to do it hard, but Ed Bernds, the director, insisted on the real thing. So, each time I hit Joe, I hit him a little harder.

"Well, by the time we're through with the shot, Joe is really steamed. And thirsty for *revenge*! Because apparently I hit him *too* hard, and he didn't like that, you see?

"So in the next scene that takes place, Joe is supposed to hit me in the face with a big cake. Well, Moe comes over and tells me, you know, 'You better watch out, because he's really gonna let you have it!' So I think, okay, I'll *brace* myself. Ed Bernds yells action, and Joe comes stumbling over with this huge cake and he really smashes me with it! Of course, I do the whole reaction, a big take and what not, and afterwards I'm going around like he really got me but *good*. And Joe is walking around, with that big cigar of his, smiling, looking all around, brushing off his hands like he really fixed my wagon! So that was his way, I guess, of evening the score."

Chapter Twenty:
"I Dunno, Norman—I Don't Think It'll Work Without the Haircuts . . . "

Shortly after the release of "The New Three Stooges" to TV, the boys began receiving fewer and fewer offers for appearances in the media or for live stage work. By the late 1960s, the Stooges were in the midst of a major popularity slump. Kids who enjoyed them on TV in the late 1950s and early '60s were beginning to outgrow them, and the trio was no longer the hottest comedy act around. (Remember, this was well before these same kids were full-fledged adults with newfound appreciation for the team's antics.)

"By 1967, you couldn't even book us in a bowling alley," confides Joe DeRita.

Moe's son-in-law, manager and producer Norman Maurer, loyally attempted to dig up work for them, but gigs were few and far between for a "kiddie" comedy act consisting of three refugees from vaudeville. Besides—by 1967 Moe was 70 years old, and Larry was no spring chicken either, so there was little point in trying to ramrod the Stooges down producers' throats.

But a TV project idea had been festering in the Stooges' minds for years—since the late 1950s, as a matter of fact. A series of Three Stooges travelogues. The Stooges touring the globe, wreaking havoc wherever they go. A veritable "kook's tour."

Norman and the Stooges put up their own cash for the production of a pilot film titled, appropriately enough, *Kook's Tour* (1969). The film was shot on location throughout California and in a couple of neighboring states. This lost episode turned out to be the Stooges' final film appearance as a team. And for years it has remained as "lost" an episode as their very first film, *Soup to Nuts*.

Kook's Tour is, essentially, a legitimate travelogue with comedy trimmings. And, like most travelogues, it features gorgeous scenery, pleasant stock music, and very little excitement. If you're expecting Moe, Larry, and Curly Joe to provide some laughs, you're in for a disappointment. The gags are few and far between, at least by Three Stooges standards, and most of the comedy that *is* attempted either doesn't make sense or is so childishly predictable it won't even hold the interest of a five-year-old.

The premise behind the "tour" is that Moe,

115

Larry, and Joe are sick and tired of Stoogeing for a living and decide to finally call it quits. They dress normally, comb their hair like useful members of society, and decidedly lay off the hitting, poking, and gouging. The boys, now full-fledged retirees, hit the road in a van to explore such tourist favorites as Idaho's Snake River and Wyoming's Grand Tetons National Park. Accompanying the Stooges on the journey is Norman Maurer's dog Moose, an affable, well-trained pet essentially playing himself.

Moose, however, is about the only character in the film with any real physical energy. Moe, with dyed, slicked-back hair and Larry "Bud" Melman glasses, seems haggard and a little uneasy out of "character." Larry is as flighty and demure as ever, and, in fact, his lack of discernible personality is so ingrained now it actually *plays* like a personality. Joe DeRita seems just along for the ride, looking hilariously incongruous in contemporary western garb with cigar and pot belly as big as all outdoors. The

Producer Norman Maurer (manning TV camera) ran the Stooges' business affairs until the team disbanded in 1969.

Stooges as a unit invite comparisons to The Sunshine Boys, and not because they work like a well-oiled machine. The boys are so tired-looking it appears as if they really *are* on vacation, and somebody just happened to have a movie camera on hand to capture the fun.

Behind the "fun" of *Kook's Tour* was an attempt to showcase the Stooges in a less-frenetic-than-usual atmosphere. But the film is so laden with dull, Stooges-free nature footage that it serves only to underscore the lackluster performances of the boys themselves. A good deal of *Kook's Tour* is footage of trees, lakes, and mountains, with voice-over narration by Moe delivered in an "isn't nature wonderful"-type approach.

Nature might indeed be wonderful, but the script of *Kook's Tour* is, sadly enough, embarrassingly un-derful. For example, we find the Stooges fishing in half a dozen different scenes, with everyone catching something except Larry. While Moe, Curly Joe, and even Moose are each successful in reeling in a big one, Larry goes without a bite through most of the story. As Moe puts it, "If you don't catch 'em, you don't eat 'em." Larry is forced to eat dry corn flakes while his selfish partners feast on fish. The payoff to this lengthy running gag comes when Larry's lure-filled hat falls into the water, finally attracting some nibbles.

Occasionally, though, the script doesn't even make sense. In one scene, Larry dons Ramboesque camouflage makeup and fatigues and goes stumbling through the woods while his panic-stricken partners look for him. At one point Larry positions himself directly behind Moe and Joe as they frantically scream out his name, yet he says nothing in reply. His pals each exit in different directions to continue their search while Larry, dumbfounded, looks into the camera and gives us a shoulder-shrug.

There's more incongruous stuff that some fans might enjoy for its sheer camp value, like a shot in which Curly Joe wipes out on his minibike and some speeded-up paddleboat footage in which the boys' action isn't even readable.

Legitimately, though, trivia buffs will get a kick out of seeing Moe Howard's family throughout the film. In one scene, daughter Joan How-

"I'd like to tell a joke, Dave . . .

"But if you keep interrupting me . . .

"It's only gonna get *this big* a laugh." Moe tries to be funny despite Dave Barry in "Strictly for Laffs."

Believe it or not, Joe DeRita was a Stooge for a longer consecutive period than either Curly, Shemp, or Joe Besser. This shot was taken a full ten years before production began on *Kooks' Tour* (1969).

ard Maurer smacks Curly Joe with her purse when he accuses her of littering. Norman and son Michael (Moe's grandson) appear in another scene as littering campers who get their tent pulled down by Joe. And keep your eyes on the credits, too, because Michael is cited as second cameraman, while Joan is credited for "wardrobe," despite the fact that everyone wears the same civilian clothes throughout.

The story closes with Moe, back at home, setting up a sequel trip to Japan. "Sayonara," says the elder statesman of slapstick, as the scene fades to black. And "sayonara" to the Three Stooges after forty years of moviemaking; *Kook's Tour* would be their last appearance together as a team.

During production of the film, Larry Fine suffered a stroke and became incapacitated. Unfortunately, there was more footage that needed to be shot, so producer-director-writer

Norman Maurer, conscientious about the Stooges' investment in the project, struggled to complete the film without Larry. According to Citadel Press's *The Three Stooges Scrapbook*, Norman even doubled for Larry in a couple of instances, such as substituting his own hands for Larry's in close shots of corn flakes being crunched up in a bowl.

But despite Maurer's worthy efforts, *Kook's Tour* remains a rather pathetic swan song to the Stooges' forty-five-year career. The quality of the film, both creatively and technically, is on a par with a well-made home movie. It was, however, released for home viewing by a company called Cartravision in the late 1970s, but is no longer on the market. Contact the Three Stooges Fan Club for details on how to get your hands on a copy; chances are someone in the club's registry might have a copy they're willing to sell or trade.

Moe always preferred comedy
with a little bit of bite in it.

When a man gets hit with a whipped-cream pie, there are always three likely suspects nearby. The Stooges disrupting pal Danny Thomas during the taping of "What Makes People Laugh?" (NBC-TV, 1965).

The Lost Episodes Filmography

Below is a complete (to our knowledge) listing of the "lost" episodes of the Three Stooges, both collectively and individually. Not included are films that are frequently aired on television. Asterisk indicates lost footage *only* from episodes currently in TV release.

THE LOST EPISODES OF THE THREE STOOGES

Title of Episode	Production Co. and/or Distributor	Year of Release
Soup to Nuts	Fox	1930
Hollywood on Parade	Paramount	1933
Nertsery Rhymes	MGM	1933
Beer and Pretzels	MGM	1933
Hello, Pop!	MGM	1933
Plane Nuts	MGM	1933
Turn Back the Clock	MGM	1933
Meet the Baron	MGM	1933
Dancing Lady	MGM	1933
The Big Idea	MGM	1934
Fugitive Lovers	MGM	1934
Hollywood Party*	MGM	1934
Myrt and Marge	Universal	1934
The Captain Hates the Sea	Columbia	1934
Movie Maniacs*	Columbia	1934
Three Sappy People	Columbia	1939
From Nurse to Worse*	Columbia	1940

Cuckoo Cavaliers*	Columbia	1940
Time Out for Rhythm	Columbia	1941
So Long, Mr. Chumps*	Columbia	1941
Sock-a-Bye Baby*	Columbia	1942
Rockin' in the Rockies	Columbia	1945
Three Loan Wolves*	Columbia	1946
Texaco Star Theater	NBC-TV	1948
Jerks of All Trades	ABC-TV	1949
The Ed Wynn Show	CBS-TV	1950
The Kate Smith Hour	NBC-TV	1950
Texaco Star Theater	NBC-TV	1950
The Kate Smith Hour	NBC-TV	1951
The Colgate Comedy Hour	NBC-TV	1951
The Frank Sinatra Show	CBS-TV	1952
The Eddie Cantor Comedy Theatre	Syndicated	1955
The Steve Allen Show	NBC-TV	1959
Masquerade Party	CBS-TV	1959
The Steve Allen Show	NBC-TV	1959
The Steve Allen Show	NBC-TV	1959
The Three Stooges Scrapbook	Normandy Prod.	1959
The Frances Langford Show	NBC-TV	1960
The Ed Sullivan Show	CBS-TV	1961
Here's Hollywood	NBC-TV	1961
Play Your Hunch	NBC-TV	1961
The Tonight Show	NBC-TV	1962
The Ed Sullivan Show	CBS-TV	1963
The Ed Sullivan Show	CBS-TV	1963
What Makes People Laugh?	NBC-TV	1965
Off to See the Wizard	ABC-TV	1967
The Joey Bishop Show	ABC-TV	1968
The Joey Bishop Show	ABC-TV	1969
Kook's Tour	Normandy Prod.	1969

THE LOST EPISODES OF MOE HOWARD WITHOUT THE STOOGES

Title of Episode	Production Co. and/or Distributor	Year of Release
Give a Man a Job	MGM	1933
Broadway to Hollywood	MGM	1933
Jailbirds of Paradise	MGM	1934
Doctor Death, Seeker of Souls	Cinerama	1973

THE LOST EPISODES OF LARRY FINE WITHOUT THE STOOGES

Title of Episode	Production Co. and/or Distributor	Year of Release
Stage Mother	MGM	1933

THE LOST EPISODES OF SHEMP HOWARD WITHOUT THE STOOGES

Title of Episode	Production Co. and/or Distributor	Year of Release
Salt Water Daffy	Vitaphone	1933
In the Dough	Vitaphone	1933
Close Relations	Vitaphone	1933
Here Comes Flossie	Vitaphone	1933
How'd Ya Like That?	Vitaphone	1934
Mushrooms	Vitaphone	1934
Pugs and Kisses	Vitaphone	1934
Henry the Ache	Van Beuren	1934
Very Close Veins	Vitaphone	1934
Corn on the Cop	Vitaphone	1934
Knife of the Party	Van Beuren	1934
I Scream	Vitaphone	1934
Art Trouble	Vitaphone	1934
My Mummy's Arms	Vitaphone	1934
Dare Devil O'Dare	Vitaphone	1934
Smoked Hams	Vitaphone	1934
Dizzy and Daffy	Vitaphone	1934
A Peach of a Pair	Vitaphone	1934
His First Flame	Vitaphone	1935
Why Pay Rent?	Vitaphone	1935
Serves You Right	Vitaphone	1935
On the Wagon	Vitaphone	1935
The Officer's Mess	Vitaphone	1935
Convention Girl	First Division	1935
While the Cat's Away	Vitaphone	1936
For the Love of Pete	Vitaphone	1936
Absorbing Junior	Vitaphone	1936
Here's Howe	Vitaphone	1936
Punch and Beauty	Vitaphone	1936
The Choke's on You	Vitaphone	1936
The Blonde Bomber	Vitaphone	1936
Kick Me Again	Vitaphone	1937
Taking the Count	Vitaphone	1937
Hollywood Round-up	Columbia	1937
Headin' East	Columbia	1937
Home on the Rage	Columbia	1938
The Glove Slingers	Columbia	1939
Money Squawks	Columbia	1940
Boobs in the Woods	Columbia	1940
Millionaires in Prison	Columbia	1940
Pleased to Mitt You	Columbia	1940
Road Show	Hal Roach Studios	1940
Farmer for a Day	Columbia	1943
Pick a Peck of Plumbers	Columbia	1944
Open Season for Saps	Columbia	1944
Three of a Kind	Monogram	1944

Crazy Knights	Monogram	1944
Off Again, On Again	Columbia	1945
Where the Pest Begins	Columbia	1945
Trouble Chasers	Monogram	1945
A Hit with a Miss	Columbia	1945
Mr. Noisy	Columbia	1946
Jiggers, My Wife	Columbia	1946
Society Mugs	Columbia	1946
Bride and Gloom	Columbia	1947

THE LOST EPISODES OF CURLY HOWARD WITHOUT THE STOOGES

Title of Episode	Production Co. and/or Distributor	Year of Release
Roast Beef and Movies	MGM	1933
Jailbirds of Paradise	MGM	1934

THE LOST EPISODES OF JOE BESSER WITHOUT THE STOOGES

Title of Episode	Production Co. and/or Distributor	Year of Release
Cuckoorancho	Columbia	1938
Hey, Rookie!	Columbia	1944
Eadie Was a Lady	Columbia	1945
Talk About a Lady	Columbia	1946
Waiting in the Lurch	Columbia	1949
Joe Palooka Meets Humphrey	Monogram	1950
Dizzy Yardbirds	Columbia	1950
Fraidy Cat	Columbia	1951
Aim, Fire, Scoot	Columbia	1952
Caught on the Bounce	Columbia	1952
Spies and Guys	Columbia	1953
A Day in the Country	Lippert	1953
The Fire Chaser	Columbia	1954
G.I. Dood It	Columbia	1955
Hook a Crook	Columbia	1955
Army Daze	Columbia	1956

THE LOST EPISODES OF JOE DeRITA WITHOUT THE STOOGES

Title of Episode	Production Co. and/or Distributor	Year of Release
The Doughgirls	Warner Brothers	1944
The Sailor Takes a Wife	MGM	1945
Slappily Married	Columbia	1946
People Are Funny	Paramount	1946
The Good Bad Egg	Columbia	1947
Wedlock Deadlock	Columbia	1947
Jitter Bughouse	Columbia	1948

Index